The Primal Chorus

of

the Sacred Wood

in T.S. Eliot's

The Waste Land

W. K. BRANNIGAN

ālep press

ISBN 978-1-7385265-1-2

Published by

 ālep press

aleppress.com

Cover typography: Caslon Old Face
(typeface of 1st edition of *The Waste Land*)

Book typography: Garamond Premier Pro

Front Cover: *The Vigil of Venus* (Pervigilium Veneris)
Etching John Buckland Wright 1939
(*V. Pervigilium Veneris*, Notes on the Waste Land 428)

Proto-Indo-European schema courtesy Jack Lynch, Rutgers University

For Lorcan

and for Michael, Martin, Joe, and Steve

Whoever has approved this idea of order, of the form of European, of English literature will not find it preposterous that the past should be altered by the present as much as the present is directed by the past. And the poet who is aware of this will be aware of great difficulties and responsibilities.

(T.S. Eliot, 'Tradition and the Individual Talent' in *The Sacred Wood*, 1920)

"Poetry, music, and dancing constitute in Aristotle a group by themselves, their common element being imitation by means of rhythm — rhythm which admits of being applied to words, sounds, and the movements of the body" ... Aristotle was accustomed to dramatic performances only in rhythmic form and that therefore he was not called upon to determine how far the catharsis could be effected by the moral or intellectual significance of the play *without* its verse form and proper declamation ... The drama was originally ritual; and ritual, consisting of a set of repeated movements, is essentially a dance. It is a pity that Dr. W. O. E. Oesterley, who has written an excellent study of primitive religious dances, did not pursue the dance into drama. It is also a pity that he falls into the common trap of interpretation, by formulating intelligible reasons for the primitive dancer's dancing ... The reason may be the long continued drought. The next generation or the next civilization will find a more plausible reason for beating a drum. Shakespeare and Racine — or rather the developments which led up to them — each found his own reason. The reasons may be divided into tragedy and comedy. We still have similar reasons, but we have lost the drum.

(T.S. Eliot 'The Beating of a Drum' 1923)

CONTENTS

INTRODUCTION

The first book in this series looks at Eve, Adam and Satan in Part III of *The Waste Land*. It explores the relationship between the 'young man carbuncular' of the poem, the carbuncle eyes of Satan in John Milton's *Paradise Lost*, and the sacred carbuncle gem in the Church of St. Magnus the Martyr. In that London temple, the gem is worn by the high priest Aaron in a portrait on the altarpiece. Christianity added symbolic range by linking it with Christ, and in that respect the gem is said to throw light into the darkness. This darkness is brought to the poem as the pustular clerk visits the typist at the 'violet hour' of dusk, in the same way Milton's malevolent Satan stalks Eve in Eden. The book shows how the pustular clerk embodies a scribal lineage that reaches back to the Old Testament, to the moment scribes created the seditious Eve. Eliot terms it a mythology better 'left in the Book of Genesis'. For millennia, that myth has labelled women as inferior and untrustworthy, so requiring male supervision. To the extent that the pustular clerk represents the egoist thought systems of modernity as the terminus of millennia of such scribal Adamic supremacy, he becomes the dark Adam of modernity who assaults the typist as Eve, and as all women.

In the Notes, Eliot states that 'all the women are one woman'. By the time this woman reaches modernity, she is the typist of *The Waste Land*, isolated, alienated, and mute with exhaustion. She now contends with both the legacy of the Old Testament and with the sustained misogyny of the preeminent modern philosophy of egoism, that of Friedrich Nietzsche. A great contrast is set up in the poem between the bleak modern circumstances of the typist and the glories of womanhood, secular and divine, in previous times. The poem opens with Aphrodite, the Roman Venus, and the most important scribe to oppose the puritanical world of Milton in Part III of the poem is Sappho, the preeminent poet-songstress of the classical world. In Part V of the poem, the reader is also introduced to the *Vigil of Venus*, a festival of beauty and grace exclusive to women as they welcome spring.

In creating that contrast Eliot journeys back in time, in the schema of the poem, to the route first travelled by classical culture to Roman Britain across Londinium Bridge. He visits the cultures of the north and southern Mediterranean, exploring their roots in such entities as Aphrodite of April, adopted by the Greeks from the Phoenicians of the southern shores, and Mnemosyne of 'Memory', the mother of the Boeotian muses of more ancient oral culture.

This book follows the poem to the dawn of human culture and language, tracing the question of what it means to be an individual in society back to its tribal fireside genesis. We turn to the opening of *The Waste Land* to see how Eliot represents the genesis of culture, hearing the primal beats of humankind as Eliot figuratively reconstructs the emergence of rhythm, dance and music. Those primal rhythms include the idea of the 'first' language, Proto-Indo-European, from which many of the languages of the northern hemisphere emerged. That evolving tree of language is another poetic continuum, as the 'primitive' opening of *The Waste Land* is again connected to the modernity of Part III, further revealing the workings of the mythic layer that unifies the poem.

Following visits to the primeval cave sanctuary and the fireside sacred dance, we look at the traces of such early human culture in the Old Testament. Eliot's poetic representations of how humans came to know rhythm, and how that incited dance, are shown to evolve into the classical Greek chorus. Other aspects of the relationship between myth and modernity are explored through the Fisher King of Arthurian legend, James Joyce's palaeolithic priest, and Charles

Baudelaire's cadaverous Jesus as a form of the Hanged Man of Eliot's poem. We then return to early human language to look at the rise of the 'I', the first-person pronoun, a poetic exploration of the evolution of the human ego. In all this, the exploration of two opposing drives in humans continues, the tension between the desire for order and the taste for destruction.

Some disclaimers. This is early-stage research. While the Proto-Indo-European content of the poem, particularly the opening, seems compelling, it may be that individual instances of interpretation might be challenged. I am keen to be corrected. The same is to be said of the analysis of poetic meter and form in this book. In the essay on James Joyce's *Ulysses*, the priest figure mocked on the opening page is shown to also embody Aaron, the first high priest. Since Aaron wears the carbuncle gem in the Church of St. Magnus the Martyr, the London temple in Eliot's poem, it reflects on the conversation between these two works. Neither the 1988 *Ulysses Annotated* nor the 2022 *Annotations to James Joyce's Ulysses* list this aspect.[1] However, work on Joyce is voluminous and this may have been noted elsewhere. Again, I am keen to be corrected and read such work.

Some quotes in the first book of this series are again quoted here. That has been kept to a minimum, but is necessary since the poem is one of the most intensely distilled and compressed works in literature.

1. Primeval Modernists

H.D., Mirrlees, Pound, Stravinsky, Gorodetsky and Joyce

> The causes of resemblance between contemporaries must be
> of three kinds: the common heritage of culture at the same
> time, common exposure to the same influences at the time,
> and their influence upon each other, both of personality
> and thought and of technique.
>
> (Eliot *Clark Lecture I* 1926)[2]

T.S. Eliot was not the first to represent ancient sounds, rhythms
and culture in modernist literature. The pervasive focus on primeval cultural origins in anthropology and related disciplines in
the 1900s was echoed by many writers. Much of this poetry was
written in London, influenced by French poetry. At Eliot's request,
his friend, advocate and editor Ezra Pound wrote to Eliot's father
in 1915 'as some sort of apologia for the literary life in general',
explaining that regarding 'his coming to London anything else is a
waste of time and energy. No one in London cares a hang what is
written in America.'[3]

Hilda Doolittle was also in London. From Pennsylvania, she was
Pound's fiancé for a short time, shortened her pen name to H.D. on
his suggestion, and created the Imagist movement with him. Eliot
thought Imagism a significant moment. 'The *point de repère* usu-
ally and conveniently taken, as the starting-point of modern poetry,
is the group denominated "imagists" in London about 1910. I was
not there. It was an Anglo-American group ... a movement which,
on the whole, is chiefly important because of the stimulus it gave

to later developments'.[4] Pound described the image as 'an intellectual and emotional complex in an instant of time', and published a collection titled *Des Imagistes* in 1914. The French title reflects his comment that the 'important work of the last twenty-five years has been done in Paris'. Imagists stepped back from narrative forms of poetry prevalent since the romantics in favour of distilled intensity, to be achieved through a craft heightened by economy of language and the use of imagery.[5]

On the one hand, Eliot did not need such movements. Pound commented that Eliot 'has actually trained himself *and* modernized himself *on his own*. The rest of the *promising young* have done one or the other, but never both.'[6] On the other hand, Langdon Hammer's comment that 'Imagist aesthetics in general ... depend on the radical compression of language and the conversion of the prosaic and everyday to the essential' can be seen in *The Waste Land* in scenes such as those between the typist and clerk and Albert and Lil.[7] Further distillation and compression is achieved through Eliot's use of the shorthand of the mythic method, engaging the mythic lodes embedded in imagery such as the carbuncle gem, Satan, Eve and Adam, and Sappho's evening star. In that, Eliot adds exponential symbolic intensity to Pound's dictum that the image should incite an intellectual and emotional complex in an instant of time.

Like Eliot, H.D. was a great admirer of Sappho and emulated her muse in poetry. She wrote deliberate fragments, reflecting the destruction of Sappho's poetry by zealots and holding a mirror to the experiences of modern women. The structure of her poetry, like that of Eliot, contributes to the story. A significant aspect of her 1919 poetry collection *Hymen* — the god of marriage and one of the Erotes, the winged gods of love who accompanied Aphrodite — is a recuperation of female spirituality from ancient ritual. Resonating with the

Vigil of Venus [428n] as women-centred poetry, it opens with rituals in the temple of Hera.[8] Aspects of classical performance and ritual are emphasised through dramatic prose descriptions, mingling with ancient theatre and the strophe and antistrophe of the classical chorus.

'As from a temple service, tall and dignified, with slow pace, each a queen, the sixteen matrons from the temple of Hera pass before the curtain — a dark purple hung between Ionic Columns — of the porch of the open hall of a palace. Their hair is bound as the marble hair of the temple Hera. Each wears a crown or diadem of gold. They sing — the music is temple music, deep, simple, chanting notes'. Demeter appears in the next poem, invoking spring rites: 'till fire shatter the dark | and hope of spring | rise in the hearts of men'. She disavows slaughter rituals, an implicit rejection of Old Testament worship of a monotheistic male god in favour of softer rituals such as those of *Hymen*.

> Men, fires, feasts,
> steps of temple, fore-stone, lintel,
> step of white altar, fire and after-fire,
> slaughter before,
> fragment of burnt meat,
> deep mystery, grapple of mind to reach
> the tense thought,
> power and wealth, purpose and prayer alike,
> (men, fires, feasts, temple steps) — useless.
>
> Useless to me who plant
> wide feet on a mighty plinth,
> useless to me who sit,
> wide of shoulder, great of thigh,
> heavy in gold, to press

gold back against solid back
of the marble seat:
useless the dragons wrought on the arms,
useless the poppy-buds and the gold inset
of the spray of wheat.

...

Do I sit in the market place

—

do I smile, does a noble brow
bend like the brow of Zeus
am I a spouse, his or any,
am I a woman, or goddess or queen,
to be met by a god with a smile — and left?[9]

Similar poetics can be seen in Ezra Pound's *The Cantos*, a long poem of one hundred and twenty cantos he wrote from 1915 to 1962, yet never finished. Canto is Italian for 'song', and Canto IV of 1919 reconstructs similar ancient rhythms in 'Beat, beat, whirr, thud, in the soft turf'.

Dew-haze blurs, in the grass, pale ankles moving.
Beat, beat, whirr, thud, in the soft turf
     under the apple trees,
Choros nympharum, goat-foot, with the pale foot alternate;
Crescent of blue-shot waters, green-gold in the shallows,
A black cock crows in the sea-foam;

(Canto IV)

His goat-foot suggests Pan and his retinue of satyrs, and his seafoam is the birthplace of Sappho's Aphrodite, Ovid's Venus, and is the 'soapy sea' of Fresca in the drafts of *The Waste Land*.[10] A similar cock crows in Eliot's poem, perhaps an allusion to this canto of Pound. Since the cock stands 'on the rooftree' of the 'empty chapel' by the 'tumbled graves' [387-91], we can look to Nietzsche's killing of gods as he gazes into the abyss. 'Get up, abyss-deep thought out of my depths! I am your cock and morning-dawning ... Here is thunder enough that even graves will learn to listen!'[11]

Mathew Hollis sees a profound closeness in the work of Eliot and Pound. To read Canto VII 'is to understand something of the confluence that existed between the minds of the two poets, something of their interests and their musical ear, something in the tone of their address. It's even possible to detect a tide washing from canto to waste land ... all work converges simultaneously in a moment that is both temporal and timeless: this is the thread of tradition that binds the endless community ... Here at last was the critical concentration of all that Eliot had put before his audience. Everything was now converging in one place: the mind of Europe that lives equally in the Caves of Font de Gaume as the trenches of the Great War'.[12] In the next essays we will visit one of those cave sanctuaries of pre-history, and hear an even more ancient source for the beats of Pound's canto in the opening lines of Eliot's poem.

Reimagining ancient rituals was an international preoccupation. Sergey Gorodetsky, poet of Tsarist and then Soviet Russia, brings primal rhythm to his *Yarila* of 1919.

> First to sharpen the ax-flint they bent,
> On the green they had gathered, unpent,
> They had gathered beneath the green tent.
> There where whitens a pale tree-trunk, naked,
> There where whitens a pale linden trunk.
> By the linden tree, by the young linden,
> By the linden tree, by the young linden,

The linden trunk
White and naked.

(Sergey Gorodetsky *Yarila*)

Yarila, also known as Yarilo and Jarylo, is a Slavic fertility god akin to Dionysus, and his yearly death and resurrection is akin to that of the dying gods Attis, Adonis and Osiris of Eliot's preamble to his Notes. The poem is said to underly Stravinsky's *The Rite of Spring*, the ballet that deeply impressed Eliot in 1921, resonating as it does with the clangourous 'sounds of horns and motors' [197] of *The Waste Land*.

> The effect was like *Ulysses* with illustrations by the best contemporary illustrator ... The spirit of the music was modern, and the spirit of the ballet was primitive ceremony. The Vegetation Rite upon which the ballet is founded remained, in spite of the music, a pageant of primitive culture. It was interesting to any one who had read *The Golden Bough* and similar works, but hardly more than interesting. In art there should be interpenetration and metamorphosis. Even *The Golden Bough* can be read in two ways: as a collection of entertaining myths, or as a revelation of that vanished mind of which our mind is a continuation ... Whether Strawinsky's music be permanent or ephemeral I do not know; but it did seem to transform the rhythm of the steppes into the scream of the motor horn, the rattle of machinery, the grind of wheels, the beating of iron and steel, the roar of the underground railway, and the other barbaric cries of modern life; and to transform these despairing noises into music.[13]

In Eliot's poem there is a similar structural tension, as in a fugue, between the 'despairing noises' of the fragmented layer and the harmony of the classical mythic layer. Subtitled Pictures of Pagan Russia, Stravinsky's Ballet includes movements such as the Ritual of Abduction, Ritual of the Rival Tribes and Dance of the Earth. Its harmonies are discordant clashing tones, its melodies are elemental rhythms, and its orchestration at times is deliberately out of sync. Hollis sees similar oppositional musical intonations in *The Waste Land* through Eliot's reaction to Stravinsky. 'It would provide Eliot with the outstanding element in the long-prepared tapestry of his poem ... 'Stravinsky had metamorphosed the rhythm of the Great Steppes' into the clangour of the modern city and in doing so, had illuminated 'the final piece of the jigsaw puzzle that would become *The Waste Land* ... now it had the 'auditory imagination' within its hearing — not only the lyric melody of ragtime and dance, but the music of the primitive imagination played on modern instruments'.[14]

Primeval incantation was also reimagined in prose. *Oxen of the Sun*, episode fourteen of *Ulysses*, the organ of which is the 'womb' and the symbol the 'mother', is composed of a series of imitative prose styles in which male scribes throughout history discuss fertility, maternity, childbearing and other aspects of motherhood. It opens with a form of ritual from vegetation ceremonies in primitive incantations to the 'sun as a source of fertility' among others. 'Send us bright one, light one, Horhorn, quickening and wombfruit'. Joyce's stylistic progression 'recapitulates the evolution of prose style in literary history', from 'Latin prose to fragments of modern slang'. There is also an aspect of ritual dance that we will also see in Eliot's poem: 'turning to the right, clockwise, sunwise, a ritual gesture to attract good fortune, and an act of consecration when performed three times'.[15] It is likely that Eliot initiates a similar literary endeavour in *The Waste Land*, since there seems from the outset a map of the development of poetry from its primal sources through history to 1922.

He attempted to fill out his poem and expand it by parodying the styles of other poets, not merely in lines but in long passages. It is possible he was influenced here by the example of James Joyce in *Ulysses*, and wished his poem to go through English poetic styles as Joyce had gone through English prose styles in the section called "Oxen of the Sun." For his parodies occur according to an historic theme. Jacobean dramatists are parodied at the opening of "A Game of Chess," Pope and eighteenth-century narrative poems in quatrain in "The Fire Sermon," and nineteenth century blank verse, first person, narrative poetry in "Death by Water."[16]

Eliot maps poetry through metrical and other technical devices and allusions, and that includes the primal rhythms of a prehistoric Eurasian shared language, Proto-Indo-European. This is not an exercise in viewing primeval poetics, and later derivations such as the poetics of archaic and classical Greece, through a long lens into the past. We have seen Hollis observe that in Eliot's perspective all literary work 'converges simultaneously in a moment that is both temporal and timeless'. When Eliot describes the relationship between modern and ancient authors within the continuum of European literature, it is clear that the works coexist: 'the whole of the literature of Europe from Homer and within it the whole of the literature of his own country has a simultaneous existence and composes a simultaneous order'.[17]

In that view, literature is not only a continuum: in so far as it is available to the modern reader in written or excavated form, the old exists simultaneously with modern works. Further, where traces of the earliest human culture continue in modern culture, termed 'survivals' by the anthropologists of the time, they also have a simultaneous existence. In poetry, when poets use the works of anthropology and archaeology to figuratively reconstruct primeval poetics in ritual form through the 'broken fingernails of dirty hands' [303], the poetics and rituals of early humanity, such as the Magdalenian culture of some 15,000 years BCE, are reborn into simultaneous modern existence and effect. In that way, the primal rhythms excavated by modernist poets and writers then become part of the current order, part of the active tradition.

2. THE PALAEOLITHIC CAVE SANCTUARY

As he emerged from viewing the Upper Palaeolithic wall art in the recently discovered Lascaux caves in 1940, Pablo Picasso is reputed to have said, 'we have discovered nothing'. The cave drawings of Lascaux are those of the early Magdalenian culture of the Old Stone Age period. To visit this cave and its prehistoric artists is to see the same form of prehistoric drawings and culture that feature in Eliot's description of the essential relationship between the poet and the past, with something of the same perspective as Picasso.

> To proceed to a more intelligible exposition of the relation of the poet to the past: he can neither take the past as a lump, an indiscriminate bolus, nor can he form himself wholly on one or two private admirations, nor can he form himself wholly upon one preferred period ... The poet must be very conscious of the main current, which does not at all flow invariably through the most distinguished reputations. He must be quite aware of the obvious fact that art never improves, but that the material of art is never quite the same. He must be aware that the mind of Europe — the mind of his own country — a mind which he learns in time to be much more important than his own private mind — is a mind which changes, and that this change is a development which abandons nothing *en route*, which does not superannuate either Shakespeare, or Homer, or the rock drawing of the Magdalenian draughtsmen. That this

development, refinement perhaps, complication certainly, is not, from the point of view of the artist, any improvement. Perhaps not even an improvement from the point of view of the psychologist or not to the extent which we imagine; perhaps only in the end based upon a complication in economics and machinery. But the difference between the present and the past is that the conscious present is an awareness of the past in a way and to an extent which the past's awareness of itself cannot show.[18]

(Eliot *Tradition and the Individual Talent* 1919)

The spiritual drive of early humanity was first called 'spiritualism', before being renamed animism in part from a Victorian need to emphasise a discrimination between Christianity and such 'primitive' impulses. At the time of *The Waste Land*, those scholars such as R. R. Marett speculated that, as early humans became aware of their existence in the world, they were filled with a formless primal spirituality, a 'pre-animist' sense of awe, and a desire to express it. In his view, Magdalenian humans did so in prehistoric sanctuaries.

At Niaux, for instance, there are pictographs and paintings which, so far as can be made out, are connected with rites intended to secure good hunting. The fact, too, that they occur deep within the dark recesses of a mountain, where a certain awe is felt even by a modern mind, afford an additional proof that solemnities were being celebrated; that fine art in this case was but the secondary product of religion ... Again, at Gargas, the hand-prints stencilled on the walls possibly record some charm or vow; while the arabesques on the ceiling may have some totemic significance ... Hence we may justly speak of prehistoric sanctuaries.[19]

There is a sympathy between Eliot's perspective and Marett's, whose work he had read, marking a difference with *The Golden Bough*.[20] Frazer is at pains to discriminate between modern and primitive culture, using words like 'barbarous' and 'savage' regularly. The latter expression is unfortunately commonplace in the anthropological works of the time, reflecting social attitudes. That said, Frazer was taking a risk, writing an anthropological 'counter-bible' at a time when Establishment Church power was significant, vigilant and punitive. Thirty years later, during the completion of *The Waste Land*, that theological fervour in British culture was still evident in the battle of creeds in the Church of St. Magnus the Martyr.[21]

In contrast, Eliot sees a vital cultural heritage on those cave walls that should be honoured and preserved. In that, he is recognised as not so traditional a traditionalist. His is a 'programmatic revaluation of the English literary tradition', reshaping the concept of tradition itself. It is an 'adversarial yet reconstructive' attitude to tradition that champions a literature 'saturated in the literature of the past'. It contrasts to 'extremist modernism ... deficient in tradition'; 'several avant-garde movements — notably, Italian and Russian Futurism, and Dadaism — advocated a clean break with the past'.[22] For Eliot, the tradition is inextricable from the cultural and spiritual quest of humanity, and its starting milestone — one of many milestones in the poem — is the genesis of humankind's collective self-consciousness, its first recognition and expression of itself. In a chapter titled 'In A Prehistoric Sanctuary', Marett describes his visit to the caves at Niaux, France.

> To stand at the door of Niaux yields no foretaste of a mile-long subterranean cathedral with pillars, side-chapels, and confessionals all complete ... To post-palaeolithic man, however, the ingress to the inner sanctuary was not

improbably barred. A little way in there is a drop in the level, which rises some 25 metres on the further side, and in even moderately wet weather the dip becomes a lake. If, then, the holocene epoch was ushered in, as there is reason to believe, by a "pluvial period" of considerable duration, the chances are that the spirits of the Magdalenian men were free to carry on their mysteries undisturbed long after their bodies were dust; nay, probably right up to the day when modern science burst in upon the darkness with its acetylene lamps … There are likewise upright lines, not unlike those whereby the Australian natives represent throwing-sticks in their caves and rock shelters. Other similar upright lines have a boss on the upper part of one side, and recall the shape of a certain type of Australian throwing-club … Last of all comes a cleverly-designed little bison, the dorsal line of which is merely a projecting ridge of rock. A natural accident has been utilized — nay, has perhaps suggested the representation. This bison, unlike any other that is figured in this cave, has its legs drawn up close to the body, and this rearing position, so suggestive of a death struggle, together with the large red mark on the flank, for all the world like an open wound, makes the intention of the primitive artist passing clear. He here portrays the slaying of the bison. The other marks are presumably meant to lead up to this, and signify the weapons that are to deal the blow, the circling movements of the hunters, and who knows what besides? But why such a hunting scene at all?

The Magdalenian human was 'crossing the threshold that divides the world of the workaday from the world of the sacred; and these rites, whether the mechanism of spell or of prayer predominated in them, were genuinely religious in so far as they involved a mood and attitude consisting in a drawing near in awe, according to approved traditional usage, to an unseen source of mana.' Mana, a term borrowed from Southern Ocean cultures such as the Polynesians, describes a supernatural energy universal to all existence, animate and inanimate, similar to the spirituality of the vegetation ceremonies of Eliot's Notes.

> At Niaux we are amongst later Magdalenian artists who could, and did, draw true to life. Did they live at the mouth of their cave? It appears not. Certainly, if their art was play, they sought a remote playground, penetrating half a mile or more into the underground world ... no artist ever graved animals, or men with the heads of animals — masked dancers, it may be — for simple fun in such a place. These, then, must have been sanctuaries, if only because no one would dream of hedging round a mere picture-gallery with such trying turnstiles. The great difficulty is to make intelligible to ourselves the spiritual motives that could lead men in dark and remote places to celebrate mysteries that involve the designing of animal forms, the use of symbols, and so forth ... the artist of Niaux may have felt in a vague way that the better he drew his beast the surer he was to have at his back the kindly powers that send the spear straight at the quarry.

Like Eliot, Marett shows a sense of caution in his interpretation of this genesis of spirituality. He critiques both Frazer and Edward Tylor through that pre-animist human, whose 'rudimentary religion ... is at once a wider, and in certain respects a vaguer, thing than "the belief in spiritual beings" of Tylor's famous "minimum definition"'. Edward Tylor was a founder of cultural anthropology as a science.

In the preceding book we saw that he is named by Eliot as essential reading, and he proposed a continuum in which animism preserves an 'unbroken continuity, into the midst of high modern culture ... for where the root is, the branches will generally be produced'.[23] Marett speculates on an earlier, pre-animist stage of spirituality.

> What I would not be prepared to lay down dogmatically or even provisionally is merely that there was a pre-animistic era in the history of religion, when animism was not, and nevertheless religion of a kind existed. For all I know, some sort of animism in Tylor's sense of the word was a primary condition of the most primitive religion of mankind. But I believe that there were other conditions no less primary. Moreover, I hold that it can be shown conclusively that, in some cases, animistic interpretations have been superimposed on what previously bore a non-animistic sense.[24]

Marett's visit to the cave paintings is inflected with something of the same sense of awe and immersion of his primeval human — the ghost he meets in that cave.

> We behold a cathedral interior such as a mediaeval architect might have seen in his dreams, aerial, carven, and shining white ... Under a low vault is a snub-nosed horse, or rather pony, of grand workmanship, measuring about a metre and a half from the forehead to the root of the tail ... Away to the left the wall bends back a little above the level of the floor and overarches a small tract of sand, by this time of day coated with stalagmite, though not thickly. We stoop, and behold traced on the sand the unmistakable forms of two trout, own brethren to this morning's trout of tender

memory. At last we were in touch with the spirit of our pleistocene forerunner. He knew those trout, we knew those trout, and his emotion was ours. But a stranger thing was at hand. Hard by, similarly sheltered by an overhanging ledge, might be seen the much-bestalagmited print of a naked human foot — rather a small foot, it seemed. Silently and in awe we turned to retrace the long journey to the outer world. At last we had met the ghost of prehistoric man.

Neither Marett nor Eliot are immune to their times, using terms that would be avoided now. At the same time, both share an effort to surpass prejudices that would dismiss those outside Western society and faith as inferior humans and spirits. Eliot regards the art of the Magdalenian artists as an essential component of universal human culture, and Marett's respect is also clear. Marett's primeval threshold could be that of Magnus Martyr. It is the figurative spiritual threshold in Eliot's poem between the working day and vespers in such modern temples, 'when the eyes and back | turn upwards from the desk' [215] — the essential spiritual similarity and quest Marett sees in that palaeolithic cave sanctuary.

For man of the primitive pattern there are two worlds, a workaday and a sacred. Whenever he needs help in the one, he resorts to the other. The threshold between the two is clearly marked. He crosses it always in a ceremonial way, with nice attention to the traditional details of behaviour; and his ceremonies enhance, as they certainly reflect, the mood in which he draws near to the unseen source of his spiritual comfort. It matters not at all whether we classify as magic or religion the practices that result, so long as we recognize that all genuine rites involve one and the same fundamental mood and attitude, a drawing near in awe. Thus, then, we must suppose it was at Niaux. The man who left his footmark there had drawn near in awe, whether it was spell or prayer that accompanied his painting. And perhaps the best proof of all is that the spirit of awe and mystery still broods in these dark galleries within a mountain, that are, to a modern mind, symbolic of nothing so much as of the dim subliminal recesses of the human soul.[25]

3. The Primal Sacred Dance

The all-enveloping spirituality thought to govern the prehistoric Magdalenian culture can be seen, much later in time, in classical form in the poem the *Night Vigil of Venus*, the *Pervigilium Veneris* of late antiquity named in the Notes [428n] in which 'the wood lets down her hair in nuptial downpours'.[26] Now with an anthropomorphic goddess, a pervasive spirituality is not only responsible for all life, it runs in the veins of the celebrants. 'She, the creatress, with all-pervading spirit and hidden powers | Holds sway within the minds and the veins'.[27] The poem recreates the springtime celebration of Venus as life-giver, a three-day festival of song and dance exclusive to women.

A question of Eliot's time was whether dance came first at the dawn of human culture, as a natural response to rhythm, only later becoming ritualistic and spiritual. We will see Eliot reconstruct that primeval dance in an extraordinary way through the poetic inheritance from the first human beats. It may be that the primal rhythms and dance of his opening lines are meant to convey just that: a rhythmic urge that is the immediate response of the dancers. Eliot sees the origins of drama in such ritual, and the origin of ritual in dance. 'The drama was originally ritual; and ritual, consisting of a set of repeated movements, is essentially a dance. It is a pity that Dr. W. O. E. Oesterley, who has written an excellent study of primitive religious dances, did not pursue the dance into drama. It is also a pity that he falls into the common trap of interpretation, by formulating intelligible reasons for the primitive dancer's dancing'.[28]

Here again, in 1923, Eliot disagrees with modern projections into the primeval mind. However, he also praises Oesterley's book, attempting as it does to reconstruct the behaviours of early human rituals which Oesterley places at the tribal fire-circle. He shares with Eliot an understanding of the universal importance of the primal dance: 'the fact of its universal prevalence among all races at one time or another of their cultural development shows how essential a rite it was', though 'its origin is obviously veiled in obscurity seeing that it developed in pre-historic times'.

> Mr Marett, in the first essay of the volume already referred to, brings forward incontrovertible arguments, as it seems to us, for believing that there was a stage in the mental and religious development of man in which he was not yet capable of other than a vague sense of the supernatural; in which he had not yet associated definite spirits or ghosts with what he conceived to be supernatural phenomena; but in which the sense of mystery and consequently of awe in face of these supernatural phenomena filled his heart ... Mr Lang's "high gods" must have had a psychological pre-history of some kind which, if known, would connect them with vaguer and ever vaguer shapes — phantoms teeming in the penumbra of the primitive mind, and dancing about the darkling rim of the tribal fire-circle.
>
> (W. O. E. Oesterley *The Sacred Dance*)[29]

In the preceding book we saw Eliot named as a master-equivocator in his philosophical studies up to the time of his poem. He did not commit to 'tender-minded' idealism nor to 'tough-minded' realism, because 'my relativism made me see so many sides to questions'.[30] This attitude extends to all disciplines. He read many works of anthropology and comparative religion keenly and admiringly, while disagreeing in some respects. This includes the work of Frazer and Marett, particularly when interpretations are imposed on the ritual motives of early humanity.

Following *The Hollow Men*, his major poem after *The Waste Land*, he did make choices, most significantly in religion, and the journey to that choice is mapped in both poems. Before that, from his Harvard years through his European wanderings to the time of *The Waste Land*, he did not fully commit to any doctrine or thought system. His intellectual, cultural and spiritual quest is governed only by the *via media* and a preference for Classicism over Romanticism. He proposes the same caution in projecting motivations and thoughts on early humanity. He views such meaning as remote and indeterminate when 'in the case of religious and other social phenomena, a meaning ... hovers between the social and the individual'; and cautions that words like 'worship may describe to an uncertain degree of primitiveness; beyond that it will be an increasingly dubious interpretation'.[31]

Some years ago, in a paper on "The Interpretation of Primitive Ritual," I made an humble attempt to show that in many cases no interpretation of a rite could explain its origin. For the meaning of the series of acts is to the performers themselves an interpretation; the same ritual remaining practically unchanged may assume different meanings for different generations of performers; and the rite may even have originated before "meaning" meant anything at all. The persons concerned may believe that the ritual is performed in order to induce a fall of rain; but this innocent belief throws no light on the genesis of their behaviour; and it is true even for the participants only in that if they became convinced that the rite had no effect upon the weather, they would probably, though with regret, cease the practice.[32]

A notable aspect of Oesterley's book is that he engages with evidence of ancient dance in the Old Testament, holding as it does traces of more ancient sources. In 'the following discussion on the sacred dance we have made the Old Testament our starting-point'. In his view, the 'Old Testament offers, either explicitly or implicitly, as we hope to show, evidence of the existence among the ancient Israelites of most of the typical sacred dances of antiquity ... From this we are often able to discern, with tolerable probability, the early underlying ideas which prompted the performance of the type of dance in question; for, as may well be supposed, it is not from the Israelites that we can expect to discover, excepting in the one case of the ecstatic dance, the root motives of the different types of the sacred dance'. Under the title 'Types of the Sacred Dance of the Israelites' he lists the sacred processional dance, the encircling of a sacred object, the ecstatic dance, sacred dances at vintage and harvest festivals, dances in celebration of victory, and the sacred dance as circumcision rite, as marriage rite, and as burial or mourning rite.[33]

The evening song of vespers is of Hebrew provenance, and church processions such as those in the Church of St. Magnus the Martyr are derivations of Old Testament Aaronic ritual. There is a yearly procession from the church to the bridge to bless the River Thames, during which a votive offering is thrown into the water to protect those who work on it, resonating with rituals even more ancient than the Old Testament. The same is to be said of *Stella Maris*, Sappho's evening star as protector of those at sea who is both the Christian Mary and, as the Mediterranean Queen of Heaven, is older than Aphrodite. In the schematics of the anthropology and comparative religion of

Eliot's time, all such modern rituals — not only in religion but within culture and art — are informed by 'survivals', traces of the culture and spirituality of primeval humanity. Marrett, Oesterley and Eliot see those ritual origins in a pure, primal spirituality that envelops and flows through the world and the group, from which the individual is as yet dimly distinguished. The dance that Oesterley traces from earliest humanity is one form of the continuums found in Eliot's poem. The Hebrew priest of the Old Testament was a participant in that dance, since Frazer notes that the 'Hebrew prophets employed music in order to bring on the prophetic trance'.[34]

4. The Hebrew Legacy from Animism

Dido, Phlebas, and Canaanite Christianity

> The Christian church is an encyclopaedia of prehistoric
> cults and conceptions of the most diverse origin, and that
> is why it is so capable of proselytising ... It is not what is
> Christian in it, but the universally heathen character of its
> *usages*, which has favoured the spread of this world-religion;
> its ideas, rooted in both the Jewish and Hellenic worlds,
> have from the first known how to raise themselves above
> national and racial niceties and exclusiveness as though they
> were merely prejudices.
>
> (Nietzsche, *Daybreak*)[35]

Nietzsche's continuum between pagan, Hebrew and Christian the-
ologies is central to Frazer's *The Golden Bough* and Weston's *From
Ritual to Romance*, the books Eliot names in the preamble to the
Notes, and is reiterated in other anthological works of the time.
The Judeo-Christian version of these anthropological traces survive
in the carved foliage of the Magnus Martyr altarpiece, suggesting
outdoor worship prior to temple building and the rise of the idea
of sacred wood from animism, when the tree itself was inspirited.
There are also traces of this legacy in the Jewish Passover, marking
the Israelite transition from a pastoral nomadic culture to a more
settled way of life.

Moses orders each Israelite to perform a ritual action, and
this action will protect them from the slaughter. The ritual

consists of two parts. Each family is told to sacrifice a lamb. The lamb will then be eaten as a family meal, and its blood will be smeared on the doorposts to mark the house so the angel of death knows to pass over that house, — and the pun works in Hebrew, as well as English, which is kind of handy. In addition, each family is to eat unleavened bread. So according to *Exodus*, this Passover ritual was established on Israel's last night of slavery while the angel of death passed over the dwellings that were marked with blood.

The story attests to a phenomenon that's long been observed by biblical commentators and scholars, and that is the Israelite historicization of preexisting ritual practices. In other words, what we probably have here are two older, separate, springtime rituals. One would be characteristic of semi-nomadic pastoralists: the sacrifice of the first lamb born in the spring to the deity in order to procure favor and continued blessing on the flocks for the spring. The other would be characteristic of agriculturalists: it would be an offering of the very first barley that would be harvested in the spring. It would be quickly ground into flour and used before it even has time to ferment, to quickly offer something to the deity, again, to procure favor for the rest of the crop. It's supposed by many that Israel was formed from the merger, or the merging of diverse groups, including farmers and shepherds in Canaan. The rituals of these older groups were retained and then linked to the story of the enslavement and liberation of the Hebrews. So you have older nature festivals and observances that have been historicized. They're associated now with events in the life of the new nation, rather than being grounded in the cycles of nature. This may in fact be then part of the process of differentiation from the practices of Israel's neighbors, who would have celebrated these springtime rituals ... and we'll see this historicization of rituals recurring again and again.[36]

Elsewhere, Hayes notes that the Hebrews were a branch of the Canaanites, as were the Phoenicians. The name 'Phoenician' was coined by the Greeks for the seafarers who brought fine purple dye made from snail shells. The Phoenicians did not call themselves that, being a sub-set of wider Canaanite culture. Language scholars see the Semitic languages of all three as initially near indistinguishable, and the Hebrew alphabet is Phoenician in origin. In that light, both 'Phlebas' [312] and the Semitic-speaking queen Dido, who is suggested through the 'laquearia' [92] of her palace, are figurative ancestors of Hebraic culture in Eliot's poem. According to Virgil in the *Aeneid* the Phoenicians built Dido's palace in Carthage and, according to archaeologists and traces in the Bible, they also built the Hebrew First Temple, the fabled Temple of Solomon.

Part of shared culture is shared myth. In the first book we saw that the origin of the Greek Aphrodite, the Roman Venus, was on the other side of the Mediterranean in the Phoenician Queen of Heaven, whose Hebrew counterpart was the Queen of Heaven in the polytheistic First Temple for centuries. This has a bearing on the presence of Tiresias [243] in Eliot's poem. When Tiresias unwisely confirms Jove's opinion that women enjoy the lovemaking of 'Venus games' more than men, Juno takes exception and strikes him blind. Eliot's note states that the 'whole passage from Ovid is of great anthropological interest', and that what 'Tiresias *sees*, in fact, is the substance of the poem' [218n]. Before he is blinded, the last thing that Tiresias '*sees*, in fact' is that co-equal divine couple. Jove states that he cannot reverse that blinding because he cannot undo what another god has done, marking a gender parity in the heavens prior

to the exclusive male God of Judeo-Christianity. It is notable that
Eliot quotes the entire passage from Ovid's *Metamorphoses*.

> At pater omnipotens (neque enim licet inrita cuiquam
> facta dei fecisse deo) pro lumine adempto
> scire futura dedit, poenamque levavit honore.

> But one god can't undo another's doing,
> And so Jove gave Tiresias the gift
> of foresight to replace the vision lost
>   (*Metamorphoses* Book III 'The Wrath of Juno', 334-336)[37]

The same anthropological lens can be turned to Dido's 'laquearia', a
Latin word describing the ornate ceilings of Roman palaces. In this
passage from Virgil, again quoted directly in Latin in the Notes,
Dido offers a prayer to Jupiter and a libation, a ritual pouring of wine.

> The lamps that hung from the golden vaulting above
> Were lit, and the blaze of torches conquered the night.
> Then did the queen call for a goblet of gold,
> Heavy with jewels, and filled it with wine, as of old
> ... as thus she prayed ...
> So saying, she poured a libation of wine on the table;
> She was the first to take a sip from the cup,
> And then to Bitias gave it, challenging him;
> ... other chieftains came after.
>   (*The Aeneid* Book I 728-45)[38]

Dido's poured libation was a sacred ritual across the classical world
and ancient Near East for millennia. Libations were accompanied
with offerings of bread and made at both shrines in the household

and local open-air shrines. For the people of Israel and Judah in their relationship with the Queen of Heaven, it was a far older and more significant ritual than the new Yahwist slaughter rituals centred in the temple elite. The tradition had tenacious longevity. At the close of the fourth century CE, St. Augustine notes approvingly that his mother Monica, on Christian advice, desists from continuing the ritual when honouring Christian saints. 'In accordance with my mother's custom in Africa, she had taken to the memorial shrines of the saints cakes and bread and wine, and was forbidden by the janitor. When she knew that the bishop was responsible for the prohibition, she accepted it in so devout and docile a manner that I myself was amazed how easy it was for her to find fault with her own custom rather than to dispute his ban.'[39]

The Bible rages against such offerings. 'The children gather wood, and the fathers kindle the fire, and the women knead their dough, to make cakes to the queen of heaven, and to pour out drink offerings unto other gods, that they may provoke me to anger' (Jeremiah 7:18). Following the destruction of such shrines during Hezekiah's reformation around 700 BCE on the advice of temple scribes, one consequence was greatly improved food security in the central temple. Wine and bread were no longer poured or left at local shrines, since the only permitted offerings were those brought to the temple — offerings now elevated to lamb and other such first fruits.

> Now when all this was finished, all Israel that were present went out to the cities of Judah, and brake the images in pieces, and cut down the groves, and threw down the high places and the altars out of all Judah and Benjamin, in Ephraim also and Manasseh, until they had utterly destroyed them all. Then all the children of Israel returned, every man to his possession,

into their own cities. And Hezekiah appointed the courses of
the priests and the Levites after their courses ... he commanded
the people that dwelt in Jerusalem to give the portion of the
priests and the Levites, that they might be encouraged in
the law of the LORD. And as soon as the commandment
came abroad, the children of Israel brought in abundance
the firstfruits of corn, wine, and oil, and honey, and of all the
increase of the field; and the tithe of all things brought they in
abundantly. And concerning the children of Israel and Judah,
that dwelt in the cities of Judah, they also brought in the tithe
of oxen and sheep, and the tithe of holy things which were
consecrated unto the LORD their God, and laid them by
heaps. In the third month they began to lay the foundation
of the heaps, and finished them in the seventh month. And
when Hezekiah and the princes came and saw the heaps, they
blessed the LORD, and his people Israel. Then Hezekiah
questioned with the priests and the Levites concerning the
heaps. And Azariah the chief priest of the house of Zadok
answered him, and said, Since the people began to bring the
offerings into the house of the LORD, we have had enough
to eat, and have left plenty: for the LORD hath blessed his
people; and that which is left is this great store.

(2 Chronicles 31)

These heaps, the profits of iconoclasm, are one aspect of the 'heap
of broken images' [22] in Eliot's poem. The tension between well fed
temple scribes and the populace can be seen in the resistance of the
people, determined in defence of their divine queen.

As for the message that you have spoken to us in the name of
the LORD, we are not going to listen to you! But rather we

will certainly carry out every word that has proceeded from
our mouths, by burning sacrifices to the queen of heaven
and pouring out drink offerings to her, just as we ourselves,
our forefathers, our kings and our princes did in the cities of
Judah and in the streets of Jerusalem; for then we had plenty
of food and were well off and saw no misfortune.

(Jeremiah 44)

In the northern Mediterranean, Sappho and her culture also retain
traces of a more ancient culture of outdoor ceremony. Her Cretan
women dance 'around a beautiful altar with light feet | crushing the
soft flowers of grass'. Such open-air altars could be permanently sited
within a sacred wood or temporary, such as those of Virgil's Aeneas
in his wanderings. When he reaches the land of the Thracians, he
creates an altar on the shore, to make 'oblation to Dione's daughter,
Venus' and other gods. He gathers 'cornel and myrtle ... That abun-
dance of green, to bedeck the altar with branches | Covered with
leaves'. Later, a more sombre altar is created. 'An altar was built to the
soul of the dead man, | Mournful with dark cypress'.

Virgil describes Carthage, the city of Queen Dido, as centred
around a sacred grove of the Queen of Heaven. We have seen that
the 'laquearia' [92] of this palace is that of Eliot's poem and Notes:
'V. *Aeneid*, I, 726' [92n].

At the city's heart was a grove, with its welcoming shade,
Where first the Phoenicians, tossed by the waves and the
    whirlwind,
Unearthed the token appointed by Juno the queen —
The head of a spirited horse: a sign that their nation
Should in war be renowned and in substance rich evermore.
Sidonian Dido was building for Juno here

An immense temple, rich with the offerings made there
And the very presence of the heavenly queen.[40]

(*The Aeneid* Book I 491-8)

In this way, the traces of more ancient ritual continue in Hebraic, classical Greek and Roman culture and literature. Numerous such altars feature in the Bible, so that Hebrew outdoor worship, although of differentiated gods, was in form derived from ancient rituals of a kind with those of Dido, Sappho, and Virgil.

> There are references to large outdoor altars constructed for general sacrifices, often burnt animals. These would include that built by Noah for offerings after the flood (Genesis 8:20); Abraham's altar erected upon his arrival at Shechem (Genesis 12:7) as well as others he set up at Bethel (Genesis 13:4) and Hebron (Genesis 13:18); and Moses' altar in the Sinai (Exodus 17:15). It seems significant that these simple "Canaanite"-style altars are associated principally with the early stories of the Patriarchs, and they were probably made simply of earth and unhewn stone, erected outdoors.[41]

As Nietzsche points out, the Bible is a repository of earlier cultures repurposed to serve the new God Yahweh. Archaeology suggests that while regionally invasive wars were constant and remarkably brutal, it was locally a more friendly and collaborative Canaanite neighbourhood than the apocalyptic biblical scribes portray. This Canaanite legacy was particularised for the Hebrews by the reformist Deuteronomist scribes, who raged against it while adopting aspects for their purposes.

> The process that we describe here is, in fact, the opposite of what we have in the Bible: the emergence of early Israel

was an outcome of the collapse of the Canaanite culture, not its cause. And most of the Israelites did not come from outside Canaan — they emerged from within it. There was no mass *Exodus* from Egypt. There was no violent conquest of Canaan. Most of the people who formed early Israel were local people — the same people whom we see in the highlands throughout the Bronze and Iron Ages. The early Israelites were — irony of ironies — themselves originally Canaanites![42]

How much of the ceremony, ritual and accoutrements surrounding the Aaron of Magnus Martyr are legacies of the Canaanites, Phoenicians and the wider Levant is a question. Whatever that, the ritual inheritance from the Aaronic priesthood represented on the altarpiece of the London temple of Magnus Martyr in 1922 forms a continuum from the eight century BCE, and likely from the millennium before that. It is a continuum entwined within culture by Eliot through the inclusion of the classical Sappho, representing the classical Greek culture that emerged in the northern Mediterranean at broadly the same time as the cultures of the Semitic peoples of the southern shores. Those are the Hellenic and Hebraic cultures interconnected from the outset, including through shared divinities, and first recorded in writing around that time using the new Phoenician alphabet of 'Phlebas' [312].

Hebrew culture emerged from within a disrupted Canaanite society. Contrary to the biblical Deuteronomist scribes, the alleged 'idolatry of the people of Judah was not a departure from their earlier monotheism. It was, instead, the way the people of Judah had worshiped for hundreds of years'. Since the pre-schism Judahite rituals and gods were in the main Canaanite rituals and divinities of the most ancient provenance, figuratively in *The Waste Land*, and quite probably actually in history and prehistory, such rituals are the legacy of the primeval vegetation ceremony. 'As should be abundantly clear by now, the passages in the books of Kings about the righteousness and sinfulness of the earlier kings of Judah reflects the ideology of the YHWH-alone movement. Had the supporters of the traditional modes of syncretistic worship won out in the end, we might have possessed an entirely different scripture ... Thus, ironically, what was most genuinely Judahite was labelled as Canaanite heresy.'[43] This commentary can be leavened with another on the exclusion of women. 'In fact ... it would not be misleading to say that the *real* religions of Israel consisted precisely of all the things the prophets *condemned* ... The male chauvinist approach of the whole history of theology, indeed of the Hebrew Bible itself, raises the intriguing question of whether women would have produced a different, and in some way better, version of Israel's history, faith, and religious practice.'[44]

There is no dying god in the religion of Yahweh. The Old Testament scribes rage against Tammuz as idolatrous. He is one of the earliest dying gods of the ancient Near East, related to Nietzsche's beloved anarchist Dionysus and underlying the Adonis, Attis, and Osiris of Eliot's Notes. The same scribal antagonism is directed against the Queen of Heaven in favour of a purely male god. The First Temple scribes who plotted the death of these gods did so broadly at the same time that the myth of the seditious Eve was first recorded in writing as doctrine in the transition from oral to written culture.

An extraordinary proposition arises, a profound heresy on the part of Eliot. It is said that the Church thinks in centuries. *The Waste Land* thinks in millennia. A seeming heresy to the orthodox believer can be argued from a more ancient and universal perspective to be a correction of an Old Testament schism, a reformation of no less puritan temperament than aspects of the English Reformation. Both schisms share a horror of imagery and a fear of the divine

female, and share the extreme language of idolatry expressed as har-
lotry. The 'little pastor' Nietzsche, agitating for a similar reformation
in modernity, condemns the cultural and philosophical idolatries of
degenerate western society with similar feminising tropes.

It is the dying god and the Queen of Heaven who are 'most
genuinely Judahite', shared with the religion of Dido and Phlebas.
Before that, they were fundamental to the most ancient religions of
the sacred woods of the ancient world. Since Christianity resurrects
the Queen of Heaven in the form of the Virgin Mary, and the dying
God in the form of Christ, who is honoured with an offering of wine
and bread, in the schema of *The Waste Land* Christianity is not only
the new religion that emerged from Judaism. It is also a restoration
of the old, a counter-reformation, since it is a resurrection of early
Semitic entities more ancient than the Hebrew God Yahweh.

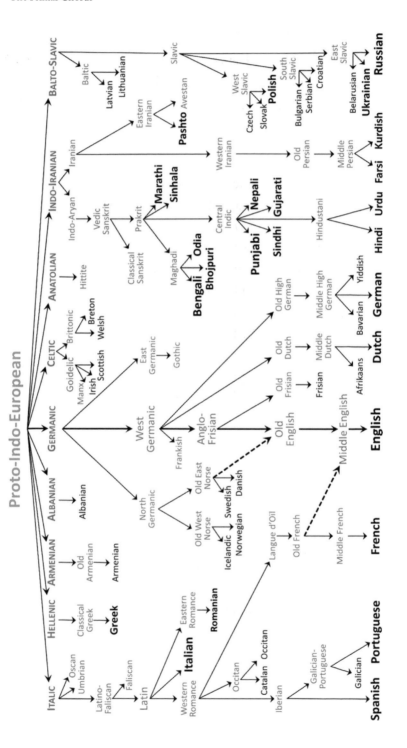

5. The Parent Language and the Prehistoric Parent Meter

In January 1922, a matter of days before *Ulysses* was published, bookstore browsers could turn for the first time the pages of Otto Jespersen's *Language, Its Nature, Development and Origin*, a pioneer summary for non-specialists of the kind of understanding out of which Joyce worked. Five decades later the principles are familiar. We are not to think of babelized languages but of Language, a mesh of filaments uniting all human beings ... The filaments run back in time likewise, binding us all to our dead ancestors ... We are joined — this is the theme of Comparative Philology — as much to one another as to the dead by continuities of speech as of flesh.

(Hugh Kenner *The Pound Era*)[45]

The philologists of the early nineteenth century, engaged in investigations that continue today in more specialised forms in sciences such as linguistics, came to realise that parent languages might underly many of the disparate languages of the world. One of these parent languages is Proto-Indo-European. It is thought to be the root language of an array of modern languages in the Indo-European language family that ranges from India to Iran and Russia and includes most of the languages of Europe. As a root language, Proto-Indo-European represents a primeval 'demotic' [212] or shared language, and has been called the first language, the parent language and the Adamic language. It figuratively resonates with the biblical story of Babel, where a language was shared by all humans before it fragmented into a babel of different languages. That babel later became the 'hubbub wide' of the city of Pandemonium in John Milton's *Paradise Lost*.[46]

According to James Frazer, much failed effort was expended by early philologists to find these linguistic origins in Hebrew: 'when the science of philology was in its infancy, strenuous, but necessarily abortive, efforts were made to deduce all forms of human speech from Hebrew as their original'.[47] They then turned to Lithuanian, the 'Lithauen' [12] of Eliot's poem. Complex yet conservative, Lithuanian was thought to have best conserved traces of its ancient roots, and so to be one of the most reliable portals to the speech of prehistoric times. The linguist Antoine Meillet, who in 1923 published *Les Origines indo-européennes des mètres grecs* — The Indo-European Origins of Greek Meter — is reported to have said that 'anyone wishing to hear how Indo-Europeans spoke should come and listen to a Lithuanian peasant.'[48]

Meillet, perhaps the most important linguist of the early twentieth century, traced the 'prehistoric parent meter' within the rise of European languages from Indo-European. 'The methods of reconstruction originally developed for recovering elements in the Indo-European lexicon were first applied to the study of meter by Antoine Meillet ... the great French philologist characterized a prehistoric parent meter deduced from ancient Greek and Vedic Sanskrit evidence'.[49] Significant for *The Waste Land*, this includes the poetics of Sappho. 'He goes on the say that iambic and trochaic Greek Verse and the Aeolian lyric types such as the Sapphic sprang from 'one and the same Indo-European type''.[50]

Meillet includes a common spiritual legacy. Writing of the similarities between ancient Greek and Vedic meter, 'he holds the resemblances between the two systems to be too close and detailed to be the result of mere chance or parallel development, and he believes that there was a certain nucleus of Indo-European meter as there was of Indo-European religion'.[51] He looks for origin evidence in philology for what Harrison sought in archaeology: a connection between the arts of modern culture and primeval humanity. 'The assumption that Indo-European prototypes underlie the metrical forms of at least Indian, Iranian, Greek, Slavic, and Celtic poetry is now respectable, thanks principally to the work of Antoine Meillet.'[52]

> Languages of the Indo-European family are spoken by almost half of the world's population, but their origins and patterns of spread are disputed. Heggarty *et al.* present a database of 109 modern and 52 time-calibrated historical Indo-European languages ... results suggest an emergence of Indo-European languages around 8000 years before present. This is a deeper root date than previously thought, and it fits with an initial origin south of the Caucasus followed by a branch northward into the Steppe region. These findings lead to a "hybrid hypothesis" that reconciles current linguistic and ancient DNA evidence from both the eastern Fertile Crescent (as a primary source) and the steppe (as a secondary homeland).[53]

Before Proto-Indo-European there were the Paleo-European languages, traces of which are thought to survive in place and river names. These include Basque and its neighbouring Aquitanian, the latter language of the Pyrenees mountains being present in the poem in a quote from Dante's *Purgatorio* [428]. Another such language forms a substrate of Greek. Before the arrival of the early Greeks to that land, a pre-Greek language was spoken of which to date, like Proto-Indo-European, no physical evidence remains. 'No written texts exist in this language, but it is known from a consider-able number of loanwords in Greek'.[54] Reconstructed by linguists from those traces, it was replaced by Proto-Greek, a daughter lan-guage of Proto-Indo-European that arrived with the early Greeks around 2000 BCE. So, the Greek word for an axe is thought to be from the pre-Greek substrate, whereas the Greek word for a hatchet is likely to be of Proto-Indo-European origin. In the next essay we will find this axe in the prehistoric work rhythms of the opening of *The Waste Land*.

The idea of a parent language is enwrapped with the idea of quest, brought to Eliot's poem in such literature as that of Chaucer and Arthurian myth. It suggests that quest, spiritual and cultural, has been part of humankind's essential character since the begin-ning. That the memory of such quests continues as traces within modern humanity is embedded in the ancient entities in the poem. Among those are the earliest known muses, Mnemosyne and her daughters Aoidē, Meletē, and Mnēmē, the pre-Olympian Boeotian muses of Mount Helicon brought to the poem in 'Memory' [3].[55] We will see that Eliot also uses the traces of prehistoric linguistic rhythms remembered in poetry to recreate a ritual choral dance of primeval origin that is full of movement and energy, and does so with remarkable effect in so controlled an opening.

The complexity of the opening poetics of *The Waste Land* is such that, for brevity in the next essay, what is explored are snap-shots of the primeval, Proto-Indo-European and classical elements of the opening lines of the poem.

6. The Chorus of the Sacred Grove

> *So the melody is the first and the universal principle ...* Melody gives birth to poetry, over and over again ... The world symbolism of music utterly exceeds the grasp of language, because it refers symbolically to the original contradiction and pain at the heart of the original Unity, and therefore symbolises a sphere which exists over and above all phenomena.
>
> (Fredrich Nietzsche *The Birth of Tragedy*)[56]

This essay looks at the remarkable opening of Eliot's poem, exploring how it figuratively reconstructs the genesis of human rhythm, music and poetry. It also represents the beginnings of ritual and so, in the view of those such as Jane Harrison and Eliot, the genesis of art and culture. In that view, the cultures of the palaeolithic cave sanctuary and the primeval fire circle dance have travelled from emergent human civilisation through the Old Testament and other chronicles and mythologies to modernity. That continuum was viewed in two ways at the time of *The Waste Land*, broadly represented in Eliot's comment that '*The Golden Bough* can be read in two ways: as a collection of entertaining myths, or as a revelation of that vanished mind of which our mind is a continuation'.[57] Most saw such traces as a legacy of superstitious humankind now superseded by science and rationality. Others saw it as an expression of an irrevocable human desire from its cultural genesis, with some also seeing in it the possibility of real spiritual consequence. That the theme of quest is fundamental to his poem from the outset suggests Eliot's perspective.

Following an exploration of the Proto-Indo-European roots and mythic import of the opening line, we look at how the metrical feet of those lines suggest the primal dance. That dance is controlled by a steady beat, a form of parent meter with rhythms that arise from the movement of human feet, speech, and the primeval working day. The introduction of the first human music to this dance seems to be held back until the second line, through 'Lilacs' and the pan pipes. In all this keep in mind Eliot's observation, in *The Beating of a Drum*, that the 'drama was originally ritual; and ritual, consisting of a set of repeated movements, is essentially a dance'. These early human rhythms and music evolve, by the fourth line of the poem, into the song and rhythmic movements of the classical Greek chorus and the compositions of the poet-songstress Sappho.

The Proto-Indo-European Opening Line of *The Waste Land*

April is the cruellest month, breeding
Lilacs out of the dead land, mixing
Memory and desire, stirring
Dull roots with spring rain.

The first book of this series looked at April from a classical perspective. That is as the month of the Greek Aphrodite, whose origin is in the culture of the seafaring 'Phlebas the Phoenician' [312] and who became the Roman Venus. Before April was latinised in Middle English as *apprile* it was *Eastermonað*, the Old English name for the equivalent Anglo-Saxon month. The linguistic roots of *Eastermonað* evoke another deity, named by the Venerable Bede as *Ēostre*, the goddess of fertility who took various forms across northern Europe.

The Eastertime central to Eliot's poem is derived from this name. Christian Easter is linked to Jewish Passover through the alternative name Pascha, and early Christianity calculated the time of Easter through the Hebrew lunisolar calendar that continues in use today in Jewish religious observance.

The word 'month' [1] marks that aspect of primeval lunisolar timekeeping that is the cycle of the moon. Its Proto-Indo-European root is *meh_1- 'to measure', which in turn is the base of the Proto-Indo-European suffixed form *$mēn$-s- 'moon/month', specifically used to refer to the measurement of time using the moon. This then forms the basis for Proto-Germanic *$mēnōth$- and subsequently Old English *mōnath* 'month '. The Greek moon goddess Selene was also known as Mene, also derived from *meh_1-, so that, rare among the Greek pantheon, she is of clear Proto-Indo-European origin, and may be the lunar opposite of *haéusōs 'dawn', the goddess of dawn. Her Roman name is Luna, from which the word lunar is derived, and Selene was often equated with Artemis, who we will meet soon with 'Lilacs' [2].

Ēostre is thought to have a Proto-Indo-European link to *haéusōs, goddess of dawn. The Proto-Indo-European root is *aus-, 'to shine', particularly of the sunrise, and the roots of *Ēostre* are in the Proto-Germanic words *austron-, 'dawn', and *aust-, 'east'. In that way, the first word of *The Waste Land* looks east to the rising sun as a source of life and divinity. Priests face the sacred east wall of churches like Magnus Martyr, where the altarpiece now sits, because they repeat the architectural template of the Temple of Solomon, that temple in turn repeating a more widespread ancient temple building heritage connected to the Phoenicians. The east-orientated sacred wall of that ancient temple and its likeness throughout the region is based on a more ancient form of worship inherited by the Hebrews from earlier cultures, the veneration of the sun.

'April is the cruellest month' for early humans because the earth that is emerging from winter is still barren. No food grows yet in the 'dead land', so that the only edible vegetation is 'dried tubers' [1-7]. It is the 'cruellest month' because it is the time of a hunter's diet of meat, a time of killing and butchery. The Latin source of the word cruel is *crudelis*, meaning rude, unfeeling, or hard-hearted. It shares roots with *crudus*, meaning raw or bloody. All emerge from the proto-Indo-European root $*krewh_2$- (which evolved into *kreuə*-) meaning raw flesh.

Thankfully the primeval group who open the poem have some comfort, since by now they have discovered fire. The English word breed, of 'breeding' [1], derives from a combination of the Proto-West Germanic *brōdjan* 'to brood' and *brōd-ō* 'to warm', further deriving from the Proto-Indo-European variant form of *bhreu-* 'to boil/bubble', *bhrē-*. In the third essay we saw the 'phantoms teeming in the penumbra of the primitive mind, and dancing about the darkling rim of the tribal fire-circle.' For this dance, there is finally the repetitive, regular beat of Eliot's comma at the close of each opening line, representing the primal rhythm or beat. In the schema of the poem, we will see that it evolves into the strophe and antistrophe of the classical chorus, but its origins are in the dance of early human cultures.

Dance: The One-step of Iamb, and the Step-over of Enjambment

Of the iamb and trochee it were superfluous to speak at length, for everybody, who has not a special prize to fight, admits the former as the ruling constituent of English verse, and the latter as an important and most valuable alternative.

(*A History of English Prosody* 1908)[58]

The beat of poetry, its meter, is measured in feet. One of the most common lines is iambic pentameter, a line of five metrical feet used by Chaucer, Shakespeare, Milton and many more. The English iamb is a metrical foot of one unstressed syllable and one stressed — da-DUM. This is a derivation from the ancient Greek iamb of quantitative verse. There is no doubt an immense lode of poetic subtlety within Eliot's usage, which includes the figurative aspect explored here. Pentameter comes from Greek *pentametros*, combining *pente*, 'five', and *metron*, 'measure', so, having 'five measures'. As the Proto-Indo-European root $*meh_1$ underlies 'month' [1], the primeval measure of the days derived from the cycles of the moon, so too it is the root of *metron*.

The inverse of the iamb is the trochee, one stressed and one unstressed syllable. 'April' is a trochee, and 'is the' is an iamb. The first lines of *The Waste Land* open with trochees and are then for the most part rigorously controlled iambic pentameter.

April → is the → cruellest month, → breeding
Lilacs → out of → the dead land, → mixing

Representing the most ancient most ancient of poetic beats, the iamb and the trochee echo human speech and movement. Three root meanings are proposed for 'iamb': the ancient Greek equivalent of 'banter', or conversation; a 'derivation from a cultic exclamation'; and 'one-step', suggesting walking and dance.[59] The iamb is the 'chief meter in most classical and modern poetry', and 'was thought in antiquity to be the rhythm nearest to common speech'; originally, 'the word *iambic* may have arisen from occasions on which ritual songs ... were sung and danced'.[60] Meillet sought his parent meter by working backwards, to those most basic human rhythms.

In any language, speech naturally tends towards a certain rhythm. Where it develops spontaneously and where it is not the imitation of some foreign model — and this seems to be roughly the case for the Vedic as for ancient Greek — metric consists of stylizing, standardizing the natural rhythm of the language. For those who study such a metric, the first care must be to recognize this natural rhythm on which everything is based.[61]

Of the two beats, the trochee is the faster. Used for swift dramatic action in ancient theatre, it is derived from French *trochée*, in a lineage from Greek *trokhaios*, a 'running foot'. As trochees, both April and Lilacs tip the participant into the dance we are about to see unfold in our primeval fireside group. The trochee is less commonly called the choreus, from Greek *khorós*, meaning 'choral dance' or 'dance', the root word of chorus. In that way, the first word of the poem sets up the evolution from that primeval dance to the classical Greek chorus we will see unfold in the opening four lines of Eliot's poem. In modern poetry, controlling the beat of the iamb and the pentameter is fundamental.

Swinburne mastered his technique, which is a great deal, but he did not master it to the extent of being able to take liberties with it, which is everything. If anything promising for English poetry is hidden in the metres of Swinburne, it probably lies far beyond the point to which Swinburne has developed them. But the most interesting verse which has yet been written in our language has been done either by taking a very simple form, like the iambic pentameter, and constantly withdrawing from it, or taking no form at all, and constantly approximating to a very simple one. It is this contrast between fixity and flux, this unperceived evasion of monotony, which is the very life of verse.[62]

It is worth repeating that Meillet finds their origins in the parent language. 'The metric type of the lyric song, the iambic type and the trochaic type, therefore come from one and the same Indo-European type'.[63] A second, more ancient source for human rhythm is from a time before language. Michael Spitzer sees the remote origins of the beat of human music in the rhythm of the first upright steps of wandering early hominids. Since Eliot sees the drama and its verse emerge from the primeval dance, and Nietzsche writes that melody 'gives birth to poetry, over and over again', the beat of the hominid steps of Ardi may have given Eliot the 'one-step' of the iamb of *The Waste Land*.

> 4.4 million years ago, an Australopithecine called "Ardi" stood on her legs and walked. And ever since then, the rhythm of walking has stamped human music ... the first steps put us on the path to forging links between the brain and muscular exertion and sound. Hominids learned to hear footsteps as a pattern — and what patterns give you is a sense of time ... The condition of being human — being midway between the birds in the heavens and the whales in the ocean — is where we can situate ourselves. Birdsong is as jerky as the motions of the bird. Just as whales have a much more fluid rhythm of floating through their own medium. Human music reflects walking, and this also gives humans their fascination with this metaphor that music moves.[64]

The human lineage separated from our ape relatives by standing erect as the bipedal hominin that would evolve through numerous early human versions into Homo Sapiens. 'Apeneck Sweeney', who roams through Eliot's poems prior to *The Waste Land*, represents this evolution when he 'addressed full length to shave', as he stands erect to remove the vestigial hair of the ape.[65] In Sweeney's case, the transformation into a groomed human is tenuous. His figurative poetic evolution terminates in the 'young man carbuncular' [231], of whom he is a primal shadow through his explicit presence in *The Waste Land* [198]. As 'all the women are one woman' in the poem, so male 'melts into' primal male [218n].

The remote beat of Ardi's footsteps echoes in the pulse of the iamb you hear in poetry today. The 'one step' of that iamb, the 'running foot' of the trochees April and Lilacs, and the 'step over' of enjambment create the primal dance of the opening of the poem. Five of the seven opening lines of Eliot's poem are enjambed, the poetic device that carries an unfinished line over to the following line. Among the many reasons are rhythmic flow or arrest, and a sense of movement. Enjambment is derived from French *enjamber*, 'to step over', a combination of the Proto-Indo-European *en*, meaning in, and the French *jambe*, leg.[66] The primeval dancer who steps from the light-footed trochee of 'April' into the series of 'one-step' iambic beats now reaches the end of the first rhythmic performance movement and, stepping over into the next line of the poem, steps quickly off the troche of 'Lilacs' to repeat the 'one step' iambic rhythm. In that way the opening of *The Waste Land* begins to come alive as ancient figures dance within the text, 'dancing about the darkling rim of the tribal fire-circle'.[67]

Spitzer's book is a remarkable excavation of the genesis and development of music from the emergence of early hominins. It 'moves progressively back in time, reverse-engineering music from the musical human of the early twenty-first century through the several thousand years of recorded human history'.[68] He introduces the concept of protomusic: a 'primitive, intermediate music analogous to what linguists call 'protolanguage' or 'protodiscourse'. The shift from protomusic to music 'is most likely to have happened 500,000 years ago … for reasons of social complexity'.

Notably, Homo sapiens was not the only musical archaic human. The language gene recovered from Neanderthal fossils shows that they likely had some form of language, and some argue that Neanderthals were 'intrinsically more musical than *sapiens*'.[69] Nietzsche's insight that melody is '*both primary and universal*' may be of even more scope, since music may transcend Homo sapiens to be truly universal, a common potentiality in what we now know to be numerous early hominin types. This may not only apply to music. 'Researchers have uncovered evidence that members of a mysterious archaic human species buried their dead and carved symbols on cave walls long before the earliest evidence of burials by modern humans'.[70] Resonating with Eliot's theme of a primal, inbuilt spiritual quest, the symbolism of imagery may also transcend Homo sapiens.

The Primal Rhythm: The Beat of the Axe

> The essentials of drama were, as we might expect, given by Aristotle: "Poetry, music, and dancing constitute in Aristotle a group by themselves, their common element being imitation by means of rhythm — rhythm which admits of being applied to words, sounds, and the movements of the body".
>
> (T.S. Eliot *The Beating of a Drum* 1923)[71]

Spitzer links primal human rhythms with the beat of walking as the Australopithecine Ardi of four million years ago took the first human-like steps. He also writes of the early hominin Lucy of three million years ago. Now an accomplished upright wanderer, 'Lucy's forays through the savannah forged the first links between music and journeying.' Through all the stages of this evolution, the work of survival was constant through the day, so that communal dance and song is likely to have arisen from the work of primeval human cultures.

> To have a concert requires leisure, requires money, and oftentimes, it's the aristocrats or the upper middle class who had the time to sit back and enjoy music performed for them. For most people over millions of years, that doesn't happen. So, the rule is that most music was performed functionally, as we say, "Whistle as you work." Also, it was performed in a participatory way. So there was no distinction between those who create the music and those who listened to it. It was the same people. The idea that we have a composer, we have a listener, is a purely modern invention.[72]

A striking feature of the opening lines of *The Waste Land* is the regular beat introduced by the comma before the last word of each line, a beat notable for its repetitive simplicity. The word comma journeys back in time through Latin *comma*, meaning a caesura, to the Ancient Greek κόπτω, meaning to strike or beat, to its Proto-Indo-European root *(s)kop-*, also meaning to strike or beat. The Proto-Indo-European *(s)kop-* is also the root of the word hatchet. Eliot's opening commas, in both linguistic root and textual visual form, become the rhythmic beat of the hand axe of the primeval working day.

In the first essay we saw Sergey Gorodetsky's primeval axe in his *Yarila* of 1919 — 'First to sharpen the ax-flint they bent'. The beat of the axe also reverberates through the opening of Eliot's poem. This seems the figurative moment humankind not only responds to, but also takes control of the reproduction of primal beats and rhythms. It will lead them to their first rituals, and on to the poetics of humanity that on one path will eventuate, in Part III of the poem, in both vespers in Magnus Martyr and the poetics of T.S. Eliot in 1922. In the first book of this series, we saw that such music and poetics have been handed on by the classical poet-songstress Sappho, who in turn inherited her music and poetics from preceding oral cultures. The repetitive beat of Eliot's comma figuratively represents the moment those primeval people take charge of the creation of rhythm — Eliot's beating of a drum that leads to dance and the genesis of controlled rhythm and beat in music and poetry.

Another fundamental human rhythm has joined that of dance steps in the opening lines of *The Waste Land*, the repetitive beat of primeval work, arising from a tool essential to human progress, the hand axe. This rhythmic sound is not only encased in the beat of the axe, it also sounds out from the act of toolmaking itself by the oldest known humans in Britain five hundred millennia ago, at the butchery site of Boxgrove in West Sussex, England.

It is often supposed that prehistoric archaeology doesn't deal with individual people, only societies, but that is not the case. It doesn't matter that we don't know these people's names (if they had names), because the material record can be eloquent. We can thus see that, at one locale, eight blocks were used by eight individuals. And we can surmise, from the 321 hand-axes found at Boxgrove, that tools were made as needed and then thrown away rather than carried and curated. Boxgrove was a site of multiple visits rather than a permanent settlement, so we can infer that culture was still peripatetic and ephemeral. Still, the record of multiple visits suggests that the celebratory ritual dance, which would have followed the butchering and consumption of the meat — either on the mudflat's natural performance space or far away, might have contained memories of early dances. Was this the beginning of musical memory and tradition?[73]

There is a resonance between this insight into primeval culture and Jane Harrison's 1913 reconstruction of the emergence of ritual and art from pragmatic life as it was thought to be then. She discerns the emergence of artistic abstraction from ritual, itself an abstraction of the hunt or battle.

> We have next to watch how out of representation repeated there grows up a kind of abstraction which helps the transition from ritual to art. When the men of a tribe return from a hunt, a journey, a battle, or any event that has caused them keen and pleasant emotion, they will often re-act their doings round the camp-fire at night ... in this re-enactment, we see at once, lies the germ of history and of commemorative ceremonial, and also, oddly enough, an impulse emotional in itself begets a process we think of as characteristically and exclusively intellectual, the process of abstraction ... if he re-enacts it again and again the particular battle or hunt will be forgotten, the representation cuts itself loose from the particular action from which it arose, and becomes generalized, as it were.[74]

Like technological advances such as the spear, the axe was central to human success. Such tools improved access to nutrition, accelerating brain size development and so cultural sophistication. The rhythms of its making, and of its use in skinning and cutting meats and other tasks, becomes another fundamental rhythm. 'There is also the obvious connection with rhythm, created by tapping and knapping flint cores. It is most likely the early hominins would not have intended to make percussive music by hitting stones, and they wouldn't have considered the resulting sounds 'music'. Rhythm was the accidental fallout of organised labour.'[75]

In that way, the rhythmic fall of the comma in the opening of Eliot's poem figuratively recreates the prehistoric sounds of work in cultures such as Boxgrove. The strophe and antistrophe of that primal work party — the leading voice and collective reply separated by the comma as it is might have been by the beat created by the fall of the axe — figuratively points to the primal origins of the classical Greek chorus. It is but an iamb, 'one-step', to see the primeval group finish work and, in the manner of Harrison and Spritzer, rise to celebrate the animist spirit in everything through ritual dance. The circular movement of that dance, as the word enjambment suggests, was perhaps a ritual stepping towards the setting sun and back again, as they might that morning have danced to the rising sun.

Spritzer's primal rhythms that emerged from early human wandering and work echo Meillet's parent meter derived from speech. Like the search for foundation myths by Harrison, Frazer and Weston, these are origin stories. Myth arose from such practices, populating the various genesis stories in *The Waste Land*. Sappho is also present to witness this genesis of art. The fourth line of *The Waste Land* is an adonic, the line of five syllables composed of a dactyl and a trochee that completes the sapphic stanza we will explore shortly.

In that way, the four opening lines of Eliot's poem represent a dizzying progression through time, from the genesis of poetry in primal rhythm and music to the sapphic stanza that evolved from classical Rome to the Renaissance and modernity. As said, it is likely to initiate a map of poetry that runs throughout the poem. Does it also initiate a map of the development of music? In the second line of the poem, we witness the mythic genesis of music in the pan pipes.

Lilacs: The Pan Pipes

'Lilacs' [2] as a plant species of many varieties has an ancient and venerable history. Heralding spring, lilacs bloom early and, because of this timing, are sometimes associated with Christian Easter and the resurrection of Christ. Said to originate in the Persian region of the Fertile Crescent and considered a sacred plant there, its name is derived from the Persian *lilanj*. Traveling through the Ottoman empire, lilacs reached Europe in the sixteenth century and were later carried to the Americas where, in North America, presidents George Washington and Thomas Jefferson cultivated them. A common link is made between *The Waste Land* and Walt Whitman's *When Lilacs last in the Dooryard Bloom'd*. That pastoral elegy mourns the death of President Abraham Lincoln, shot by the Confederate John Wilkes Booth for reasons including the abolition of slavery.

What is at least of equal interest to *The Waste Land* is the mythology of the lilac tree, particularly its association with pan pipes and the genesis of music. Called the pipe tree in England, lilacs are of the olive family Oleaceae and of the genus Syringa. The latter derives from Latin *syrinx*, meaning reed flute or pipe, in turn from the Ancient Greek *sûrinx*, meaning a shepherd's pipe. *Sûrinx* also translates variously as pipe, tube and quill, and denotes the hollow stem of a plant used to make such pipes — the hollow stem of the lilac.

In classical myth, Syrinx was a chaste Arcadian nymph who venerated the similarly chaste nature goddess Artemis. We have met Artemis's Proto-Indo-European doppelgänger in the moon goddess Selene. The evolution suggested from the very ancient Selene to the

Olympian Artemis from the opening line of Eliot's poem to the second is one of several movements through time in the opening, and of many throughout the poem. Artemis is also present in a later manifestation in the form of her Roman equivalent Diana, whose sacred grove opens *The Golden Bough* and whose Dianatempel, the pavilion of Diana, is at the centre of the 'Hofgarten' [10].

Syrinx was beautiful, and so an object of lust for satyrs and the nature god Pan who, hooved like the satyrs, pursued Syrinx into a river. Fearing for her chastity, she pleaded for rescue to the nymphs of the river, who turned her into a reed, a form of the suicide that presses on the mind of women in Eliot's poem. The aspect of the poem that is a beast fable starts here, part of man and poem from their genesis. The same bestial, cloven footed sexual desire is represented in the assault on the typist in Part III of the poem through the association between the carbuncle eyes of Milton's Satan and the 'young man carbuncular' [231], and in the satyriasis of the 'demobbed' Albert [140]. Satyriasis in modern usage is hypersexuality; in ancient times, the same uncontrolled sexual appetite was thought to risk physical transformation into a satyr. Denied gratification, Pan plucked the reed, and his frustrated breath playing across it brought out a musical sound, from which he created the panpipes. In this glimpse into the mythic method of *The Waste Land* we see the figurative genesis of music.

There is again an opposition to Nietzsche in his appreciation of the satyr as a necessary return to nature. Eliot's satyr is a classical representation of the beast in man, the same animal aspect of the Darwinian intelligent ape — represented by his character Sweeney, poetic older brother of the pustular clerk — that is a danger to society and the vulnerable. From Eliot's classical perspective it is culture, properly constructed, that quells such destructive animal impulses. For Nietzsche, the transgressive satyr is essential to men as an escape route from such socialisation. Jürgen Habermas sees this 'Dionysian messianism' as Nietzsche's 'escape route from modernity'.[76] As often in his work, there is a gap between Nietzsche's rigorously ordered celibate life and his Dionysian ithyphallic romantic imagination. Eliot sees Nietzsche's overman take his first steps from this satyr as he walks proudly erect with fearless gaze into the future. Nietzsche's 'sexual omnipotence of nature' is represented in brute form in Eliot's pustular clerk and, as often in Nietzsche's work, he shows scant concern for woman as Syrinx, driven to suicide by the street manifestation of his version of the virile mythic satyr.

> The satyr and the idyllic shepherd of more modern times are both products of a longing for the original and the natural; but with what firm and fearless hands did the Greeks reach out for this man of the forest, and how shamefully and timidly modern man dallies with the flattering image of a meek and mild flute-playing shepherd! Nature before knowledge has set to work on it, before the bolts of culture have been broken open — that is what the Greeks saw in his satyr, which he did not yet identify with the ape. On the contrary: what he saw was the archetype of man, the expression of his highest and strongest impulses, as excited enthusiast, delighted by the proximity of the god, as a compassionate comrade, in whom the suffering of the god is repeated, as wise prophet from the depths of the breast of nature, as symbol of the sexual omnipotence of nature ... Before him, the man of culture shrivelled up into a deceitful character.
>
> (*The Birth of Tragedy*)[77]

The figurative development of dance and music that evolves in *The Waste Land* seems to start in the opening line as the primal rhythm, with the advent of musical instrumentation arriving with the pan-pipes of the second line. The Proto-Indo-European root *(s)twer- of 'stirring' [3], 'to turn' or 'whirl', again evokes animist 'phantoms teeming in the penumbra of the primitive mind, and dancing about the darkling rim of the tribal fire-circle'. Those amorphous spirits evolved into the anthropomorphic mythos of the classical world that is now emerging in the opening of *The Waste Land*, teeming as it is with satyrs, hoofed gods, nature and lunar goddesses, the muses of mounts Helicon and Olympia, and the nature and river nymphs of Arcadia.

The first book of this series looked at another source of mythic riches in 'the violet hour' of the poem: Sappho's evening star Hesperus [221n], the planet Venus in the night sky as the classical heavenly representation of Venus and her Greek predecessor Aphrodite. It may encase another allusion, one that would mark a further connection between the ancient worlds of the opening and the bleak modern scene of Part III of Eliot's poem. That is to Virgil's *Eclogue* X, a reworking of the Greek myth of the poet Daphnis, who accompanied Artemis while playing pan pipes. Daphnis is said to be the inventor of pastoral poetry and is considered its classical patron. Virgil's poem closes as the evening star rises. 'Now homeward, having fed your fill | eve's star is rising'. That latter phrase in its Latin original is *venit Hesperus*, and is preceded by the famous phrase *Omnia vincit amor*, 'Love conquers all'. If the allusion is accepted in that context, it seems a suggestion of the potential for communal love in the shared rituals, culture and art that arise from universal drives of the most ancient provenance.

An ancient Greek wind instrument akin to the panpipes was the double-reeded aulos, often called the double flute, central to Dionysian ritual. According to Harrison, 'Dionysos is not only the beautiful young wine-god, but also an ancient tree-god'.[78] With such roots in animism, Dionysus was one of the most ancient dying gods and, as the god of wine, he facilitated exciting theatre in classical Greece. In the late nineteenth century, he becomes Nietzsche's representation of the iconoclasm and disruption of order needed to precipitate his reformation of decadent modern society. For Nietzsche, Christianity is the primary cause of such degeneracy, so that he ends his autobiographical *Ecce Homo* with the battle cry, 'Dionysos against the crucified'.

This resurrection of Dionysus as an anarchic cultural disruptor begins in *The Birth of Tragedy*, in which Nietzsche pays significant attention to Euripide's play *The Bacchae*. It was first performed at the Theatre of Dionysus in Athens in 450 BCE, in which the Dionysian chorus of fifteen women discuss the action as they circle from west to east and back, in the strophe and antistrophic rhythm of classical Greek theatre.

East to West
The Strophe and Antistrophe of the Chorus

In the schema of *The Waste Land* the ritual steps of very ancient peoples, the one-step of the iamb and the step-over of enjambment of the primeval fireside dance, later becomes the strophe and antistrophe of the classical Greek chorus as it moves from east to west and back, from the rising to the setting sun. The oldest rhythmic movements around the animist fire-circle also evolved into ritual dance around the altars of Dionysus, Apollo, Demeter, Aphrodite and the anthropomorphic deities of the early Hebrews; what James Joyce sees as 'hailhooping round David's that is Circe's or what am I saying Cere's altar'.[79] In those forms we also glimpse the ancestors of the festive women who dance in the sacred grove of the *Night Vigil of Venus*, and Sappho's Cretan women who dance 'around a beautiful altar with light feet | crushing the soft flowers of grass'. [80] This is broadly the classical moment when Greek oral culture gave way to the newly adopted Phoenician alphabet that facilitated the written music, poetry and drama preserved in history. In the opening poetics of Eliot's poem, the strophe and antistrophe of that chorus retain traces of the memory techniques, rhythms, movements and incantations of the preceding oral cultures.

The Greek chorus was a group of up to fifty women or men, old or young, depending on the needs of the drama. It often contributed backstory in précis from, voiced social and religious norms, and provided a range of other commentary on the dilemmas facing the protagonists. In response to the strophe of the *coryphaeus*, the head of the chorus, they spoke the antistrophe response in one voice, so collectively representing an observational 'character' in the drama. As a device in music, poetry and tragedy, the strophe and antistrophe can vary in length and voice depending on the demands of the work. In the opening lines of *The Waste Land*, it takes the form of a long strophe followed by a single word response, similar to an aspect of the ancient poetic form the paean, later becoming a feature of Christian liturgical recitals.

While the precise movements are not preserved in the works concerned, dance was an essential accompaniment to the song and poetry of the classical chorus, and those combined elements were ritualistic in form. This movement can be seen in the root meanings of strophe and antistrophe. The Ancient Greek *antistrophē* is a compound meaning 'return of the chorus', signifying a 'turning back' from left to right, in response to the strophe, derived from 'the turn', signifying the movement of the chorus from right to left, or east to west. The word strophe is in turn derived from the Proto-Indo-European root *streb(h)-*, 'to turn'. The regular beat of the end words 'breeding', 'mixing', 'stirring', 'covering' and 'feeding', and the opening lines themselves, suggest the strophe of the *coryphaeus* and the choral response, the antistrophe. In that way, the directionality of the opening text of *The Waste Land* becomes the dance of the classical Greek amphitheatre. The dance of culture between London to the west and the Hellenic to the east is also suggested in the strophe and antistrophe of the poem.

One aspect of the movement from east to west is that it repeats the cycle of the sun from sunrise to sunset. We have seen that April, the first word of the poem, was previously *Eastermonað*, evoking the goddess of fertility *Ēostre*, who is linked to the dawn. Like James Joyce's *Ulysses*, it is possible that within the pseudo-anarchy of Eliot's poem there is at least one of the Aristotelian unities. Since the sun rises in the dawn of the poem, and we see 'the sun's last rays' [225] as the 'young man carbuncular' arrives at dusk, all the intervening action takes place, in the timeless sense always present in the poem and throughout the work of Eliot, over the course of a day. It may be that parts I to III of the poem form three acts, from dawn to day and dusk, with parts IV and V of the poem serving in other ways. It would be a day in which woman falls from the heights of Aphrodite to the bedsit of the typist, shocked into muteness. Notably, it is at this bleak modern moment of the 'violet hour' that we are introduced to Sappho and her evening star Hesperus, the star of Aphrodite and Venus [221n], whose month is April. [81]

The Adonic and the Sapphic Stanza

That Eliot is engaging on the level of the chorus can be seen in 'Dull roots with spring rain' [4]. It is an adonic, the fourth line of a sapphic stanza, drawing its name from Sappho's *Ode to Adonis*. Here again we connect with Sappho, the muse who, through her part in shaping modern culture, preserves and transmits the most ancient cultures in poetry and music. The sapphic stanzas of Algernon Charles Swinburne's *Sapphics* all end with an adonic, a line of five syllables composed of a dactyl (two stressed and one unstressed syllable) and a trochee (two stressed syllables). We have seen that 'April' and 'Lilacs' are trochees, and that another name for that metrical foot is the choreus, from Greek *khorós*, meaning 'choral dance'. In that way, fragments of the chorus and its origins in primeval dance are found throughout the opening of *The Waste Land*. Further, the opening word of the poem is now linked to the end word of the fourth line, both trochees. In that, the map of poetry that is likely to exist in the poem begins to reveal itself.

'The sapphic has been the longest lived of the classical lyric strophes in the West. But full studies of its history in several vernaculars still remain to be written'. The complexity of the sapphic stanza cannot be addressed here save for a few comments. Its modern embodiment is not solely the form of Sappho, as it has been reworked by poets through history. It was the Roman Horace whose 'treatment of the sapphic as a four-line stanza canonized that form for posterity'. This four-line form opens *The Waste Land* and seems reworked again by Eliot, perhaps through Seneca. 'Seneca sometimes used the separate elements in a different order, e.g., by arranging a continuous series of longer lines with an adonic clausula'.[82] The adonic clausula, meaning 'little conclusion' in Latin, can be heard in the descending beat of 'Dull roots with spring rain'.

While the resonance between the opening of his poem and the sapphic stanza is clear, Eliot is not following the form exactly because, in the manner of Horace, Seneca, the Renaissance poets and others, he is reworking it for his own purposes. That includes, as he figuratively reconstructs Meillet's primal parent meter, a poetic reverse-engineering of more ancient forms inherited by Sappho. It seems that the four opening lines of *The Waste Land*, approximating to a sapphic stanza and ending precisely in a sapphic adonic, contain a history of poetry from its primeval genesis to the classical period of Sappho, and on to Renaissance and other adaptations of her poetics. In book one we saw the musicality of Sappho's poetics become vespers in Magnus Martyr, so that the 'music upon the waters' [257] that is in part the sound of vespers holds traces of sounds that have travelled the river [173] of culture from earliest humanity.

We have met Mnemosyne and her daughters Aoidē, Meletē and Mnēmē, the Boeotian muses more ancient than the Olympian pantheon invoked through 'memory' [3]. Classical scribes considered them the source of inspiration and craft necessary for the composition of poetry and song, and for subsequent recitals. 'When Greek oral culture was committed to writing we find embedded in it the mention of Mnemosyne, which is the personification of an important and vital force in oral composition. Its importance is evident in the prominent place it occupies in early Greek theology'. She and her daughters 'are very ancient figures, little worshiped anywhere in historical Greece, and belonging to a past so remote that the earliest Greeks of whose opinions we have any certain knowledge saw them surrounded with a haze of extreme antiquity. The inclusion of Mnemosyne as one of the most ancient deities is evidence of the importance in which this function was held by the earliest Greeks'. That function was recital from memory, and 'this legend preserves the primaeval importance of memory among pre-literate Greeks ... Folk-memory has preserved in this legend the once supreme importance of a divinity who sank into a minor cult with the advent of written literature'.[83]

The cultural inheritance from this oral tradition includes the *Iliad* and the *Odyssey*, and reciting either epic from memory would have been a formidable achievement. Both are now thought to have developed over time within that long preceding oral tradition, later recorded in the new alphabet acquired from 'Phelbas the Phoenician' [312] and then attributed to Homer. Those epics and other ancient long poems provide many traces of pre-Greek and Proto-Indo-European linguistics. In the manner of Jane Harrison's reenactment of the hunt, the primeval dance figuratively reconstructed in Eliot's opening poetics combines, in 'Memory', with this aspect of very ancient recital. It opens a figurative portal through which is witnessed the very earliest dance, recital, dramatic recreation and ritual of our earliest shared culture. Further, Mnemosyne suggests the retained memory of culture, as Eliot advocates the literary tradition as an example of the same retention of culture.

We may also be witnessing the earliest origins of the priest figure, a figure we will meet again with the high priest Aaron, and the hero figure who later became Homer's Odysseus and Virgil's Aeneas. At 'the darkling rim of the tribal fire-circle', the primeval heroes are the brave hunters who ensure the survival of the group at a time of a still 'dead land' [2], providing the meat that is butchered and cooked in the opening line of *The Waste Land* during the cruel month of April.

The Anti-Chorus of Pandemonium

Nietzsche saw the chorus as the 'true primal drama' of 'purely religious beginnings', and that the 'satyr chorus of the dithyramb is the rescuing deed of Greek art'.[84] We have seen Pan, the god of those satyrs, rapaciously pursue the chaste Arcadian Nymph Syrinx into a river, and her form of suicide as defence. We have seen the resonance with the similarly cloven-footed Satan of the 'carbuncle eyes' and Eliot's 'young man carbuncular'. The poem suggests that, rather than the elevated fictional overman, the pustular clerk is the more likely street manifestation of the unfettered selfishness of Nietzsche's celebration of the anarchic Dionysian, in which he lauds the satyr as a representation of the glories of a newly unleashed man, his Adam of the future. The satyr of his philosophy of extreme egoism becomes, in Eliot's poem, the brute satyriasis of the pustular clerk and the returning warrior Albert, who evokes another hero of extreme egoism, Max Stirner's unrestrained 'desiring man'.[85]

Eliot 'said it was a pity that poets hadn't learned more from choral work. 'And by choral work I do not mean simply verse to be spoken by a number of people in unison, but by an orchestration of a number of different voices speaking singly in turn.' Hollis sees Eliot's chorus in the poem as not 'a Greek chorus then, but a harmony found in consecutive and sometimes discordant parts. And not a series of unrelated images either, but a coordinated catalogue of visions that had given a title to the section: the blazing eye of prophecy, the seer, the prophet and the Buddha'.[86]

We have seen that the classical chorus is a feature in modernist literature. The choruses of H.D. and Pound, and the 'chorus (of Dubliners) that, as Aristotle said it should, functions collectively as a fourth character' in Joyce's *Ulysses*, pose a question.[87] What is the function of the clangourous chorus of the fragmented layer of *The Waste Land*? The 'multivocal, multilingual' bedlam of the fragmented layer of Eliot's poem seems a pandemonic anti-chorus, an irredeemable clangour in discord with the classical harmony of the mythic layer.[88] An aspect of that discord represents a world created by the alienating extreme egoisms of modernity, embodied in the pustular clerk. In the schema of Eliot's poem, the chorus emerged from the primeval fireside dance, and so did the human capacity for discord. It suggests that the tension between society and the individual, between the desire for order and the taste for anarchy, between the lust for power and the need for community, has existed from the first moments of culture, as humankind sought order amidst chaos.

7. THE IMPOTENT FISHER KING AND ATTIS

Jessie Weston and the Plan of the Poem

> And when there were men, in their various ways, they
>   struggled in
> torment towards GOD ...
> Worshipping snakes or trees, worshiping devils rather than
>   nothing: Crying for life beyond life, for ecstasy not of
>   the flesh ...
> Invented the Higher Religions; and the Higher Religions
>   were good
> And led man from light to light, to knowledge of Good
>   and Evil ...
> affirmation of rites with forgotten meanings ...
> Bestial as always before, carnal, self-seeking as always before,
> selfish and purblind as ever before,
> Yet always struggling, always reaffirming, always resuming
>   their march.
>
> (T.S. Eliot *Choruses from 'The Rock'* 1934)[89]

Choruses from 'The Rock" are extracts from Eliot's 1934 play *The Rock*, often published separately. The play was commissioned at short notice, with specific instructions on the scenes he was to write. In the rush to complete it, Eliot was quite direct. Perhaps for the only time in his creative work, his famed (or infamous) opacity is minimised. For that reason, the play serves as a window into the intellectual structure of his Christianity, in which he was consistent. The progression in this chorus from animism to the 'Higher

Religions' (notably plural) is a universal form of the progressive revelation visually narrated on the Magnus Martyr altarpiece, and echoes the cultural and spiritual continuums of *The Waste Land*.

The two books of comparative religion named in the Notes, Frazer's *The Golden Bough* and Jessie Weston's *From Ritual to Romance*, link ancient rituals to modern Western society and its main religion. Eliot claims that the title, the plan and a good deal of the incidental symbolism of his poem can be found in Weston's book. 'Indeed, so deeply am I indebted, Miss Weston's book will elucidate the difficulties of the poem much better than my notes can do'. He later qualified that, writing that to seek the key to *The Waste Land* in the grail element of Weston's book is a 'wild goose chase'. Weston's focus, and that of *The Waste Land* as it relates to Weston's book, is on the Fisher King. She traces the roots of the Fisher King of Arthurian legend from its later Christianised versions to origins in the fertility myths of the Ancient Near East.

Weston traces the Fisher King's roots to the Attis myth, establishing a 'chain of descent connecting early Aryan and Babylonian Ritual with Classic, Medieval and Modern forms of Nature worship'. In her view, the figure of the Fisher King arises from existing continental 'customs recognised as survivals of ancient beliefs' and is directly related to myths and rituals of 1000BC, the 'Attis-Adonis cult'.[90] Attis is central to the theme of the yearly dying god in Eliot's poem and *The Golden Bough*, where Frazer remarks that the similarities with the biblical Christ were so strong that followers of both Christ and Attis, who coexisted for an extended period, made mutual accusations of fakery and theft of the symbolic.

Noting that '*Fish-Fisher* symbolism' was commonly thought to be of Christian origin, she points out that 'Christianity did no more than take over, and adapt to its own use, a symbolism already endowed with a deeply rooted prestige and importance ... we can affirm that the fish is a Life symbol of immemorial antiquity, and the title of Fisher has, from the earliest ages, been associated with Deities who were held to be specially connected with the origin and preservation of life'. She locates versions of this Fisher figure in the Indian Manu and Vishnu, also linked to the Buddha. Elsewhere, the 'Babylonians had the Fish, or Fisher god Oannes who revealed to them the arts of Writing, Agriculture, etc., and was, as Eisler puts it, 'teacher and lord of all wisdom''. She connects such symbolism 'first with Orpheus, later with Christ', and makes a further comment that 'the opinion of the most recent writers on the subject is that the Christian Fish symbolism derives directly from the Jewish, the Jews on their side having borrowed freely from Syrian belief and practice'.[91]

In the poem, the explicit reference to the Fisher King [46n] is supported by further allusions. He is likely to inform the character who is 'fishing in the dull canal' [189], although in what way is to be determined. 'This king, known as the Fisher king, is impotent, and for that reason his land is barren'.[92] The character 'Fishing, with the arid plain behind me' [424] links the Fisher King to Hezekiah, suggested by the resonance between the next line, 'Shall I at least set my lands in order?' [425], and the Bible. 'In those days was Hezekiah sick unto death. And the prophet Isaiah the son of Amoz came to him, and said unto him, Thus saith the Lord, Set thine house in order; for thou shalt die, and not live' (2 Kings 20). That was the moment Hezekiah was afflicted with a near-fatal boil, subsequently reprieved by God. It was Hezekiah who initiated the Old Testament reformation that saw the destruction of shrines to ensure that Yahweh was the sole deity. The themes of impotency, extremism and iconoclasm, and the resultant waste land, are also linked to Nietzsche, who fishes for fellow destructive egoists. 'Included here is the slow search for those related to me, for such as out of strength would offer me their hand for *the work of destruction. — From now* on all of my writings are fishing hooks: perhaps I understand fishing as well as anyone?'[93] Nietzsche advocated a deliberate, iconoclastic waste land in the interests of a cultural reformation. 'We have forsaken the land and gone to sea! We have destroyed the bridge behind us — More so, we have demolished the land behind us! ... Woe, when homesickness for the land overcomes you, as if there had been more *freedom* there — and there is no more 'land'!'[94]

Arthurian legend is of French origin in the verse romances of the late 12th century. An oblique reference to the Fisher King arises from '*Et O ces voix d'enfants, chantant dans la coupole!*' [202], a quote from *Parsifal* by Paul Verlaine, the French decadent poet who later converted to Catholicism. Translated as 'And O those voices of the children singing under the cupola', one aspect of that reference in Eliot's poem is how myth evolved across Europe over time. Verlaine refers to Wagner's German opera *Parsifal*, an adaptation of the Arthurian grail romance *Parzival* written by a German medieval knight in the early thirteenth century. It is in turn derived from the earliest of such Arthurian romances, the French *Perceval ou le Conte du Graal — Perceval and the Story of the Grail* by Chrétien de Troyes. Combined, these trans-continental medieval romances constitute one of the major body of works in Western literature. This layering of references in Eliot's poem becomes a continental map of the interplay and evolution of European Fisher King symbolism, and to that can be added Weston's claim that it originates further afield in time and geography.

As those such as W.B. Yeats observe, Arthurian legend has many resonances with earlier, Celtic myth that also spanned Europe, a body of myth likely in turn to be the repository of more ancient myth, including that of Proto-Indo-European peoples. An essay of 1910, *The Bleeding Lance*, shows such thinking. It traces the transition of the Arthurian magic lance from its original warring significance to healing Christian symbol, including versions said to have pierced the side of Jesus.

> Students of the grail have hardly attached importance enough to the pagan atmosphere, which in the earlier grail stories clings to the bleeding lance, nor given sufficient weight to the fact that the lance is apt to be described first, and is often made more prominent than the grail ... Both Chrétien and Wolfram mention barbaric properties of the bleeding lance, difficult to reconcile with any Christian association, of which they appear to be altogether ignorant. Chrétien definitely ascribes to his bleeding lance marvellous destructive powers which are manifestly unchristian, and which put it in the same class with the malignant weapons of ancient Celtic story.[95]

Clearly connecting Attis and the Fisher King, Weston writes in another chapter summary that in 'the Attis initiation the proof that the candidate has successfully passed the test is afforded by the revival of the god — in the Grail romances the proof lies in the healing of the Fisher King'.[96] Weston characterises this as a chain of evolution: 'I found, not only the final link that completed the chain of evolution from Pagan Mystery to Christian Ceremonial, but also proof of that wider significance I was beginning to comprehend. The problem involved was not one of Folk-lore, not even one of Literature, but of comparative religion in its widest sense'. She summarises the intent of her work by stating that she has 'set forth elements that may prove of real value in the study of the evolution of religious belief'.[97]

Eliot stepped back somewhat from Weston's book in 1957, saying he had wished to use her imagery rather than subscribing to the 'validity of her thesis.'[98] That may have been due to academic challenges as the fields of anthropology and comparative religion advanced. However, Weston's ideas on the origin of the Fisher King in ancient Mediterranean myths such as that of Attis may not be entirely fanciful. We have seen that the white and gold of Magnus Martyr deliberately repeats the colours of the Hebrew First Temple. As 'all the women are one woman' [218n], the poem suggests that all the gods and all the temples are one. Recent work in archaeology has combined with ancient DNA studies to make a remarkable suggestion: that some of the neolithic people of Britain and Ireland, and their various megalithic constructions, originate in the early culture of the Ancient Near East. Those megalithic structures range from single standing stones known as menhirs, a version of which features in the Old Testament, to structures of significant size and sophistication such as Stonehenge and surrounds.

There were successive waves of migration across Europe from neolithic times to the Bronze and Iron Ages. 'DNA analysis of the Neolithic woman from Ballynahatty, near Belfast, reveals that she was most similar to modern people from Spain and Sardinia. But her ancestors ultimately came to Europe from the Middle East, where agriculture was invented.'[99] Tests on the remains of Stonehenge humans tell a similar story. 'The ancestors of the people who built Stonehenge travelled west across the Mediterranean before reaching Britain'. Further, they brought their rituals and temples. 'In addition to farming, the Neolithic migrants to Britain appear to have introduced the tradition of building monuments using large stones known as megaliths. Stonehenge in Wiltshire was part of this tradition'.[100] Jane Harrison commented on that ancient human homogeneity in 1913. 'We now know that the whole eastern and probably the western basin of the Mediterranean was, from Neolithic days, occupied by a people whose civilization was, broadly speaking, homogeneous, and that this civilization continued substantially unbroken from Neolithic down to historic days'.[101]

Weston links Attis to 'ancient Sumerian laments for Tammuz ... *Lord of the Net*, the nearest equivalent I have found so far to our Fisher King'.[102] Her scheme in which the Fisher King arose from ancient deities of Levantine seafaring and surrounds might be extended back in time. Long before the Hebrews, Canaanites and Phoenicians existed, traces of earlier spiritual belief systems from that area of the world seem to have travelled across Europe to the island that would later become Britannia. There, as in the France of romance legends, the Celtic pantheon, holding pre-Celtic mythic traces that in Weston and Eliot's time were termed 'survivals', met the Judeo-Christian belief system following its journey along the same routes later in time.

In the sea off the coast of what is now Israel, in the neolithic settlement of Atlit Yam of the ninth millennium BCE, a stone circle has been discovered, a small megalith that in simple form echoes Stonehenge and predates it by millennia. Thought to have been built around a freshwater spring, there are cup carvings on the stones. The settlement was submerged during a substantial rise in sea levels that initiated population migrations. Assuming the local survival of the lineage of the neolithic humans who remained, they later developed into such early Semitic cultures as the Canaanites, Phoenicians and Hebrews. The people who built that small megalith are termed an agro-pastoral-marine culture, thought to have practised simple crop farming, herding, hunting and gathering, and sea fishing. The symbolism of fish is likely to have been important to them as was that of water, with rituals to encourage the fresh growth of vegetation in spring.

8. The High Priest Aaron in James Joyce's *Ulysses*

Creation from nothing ... The cords of all link back,
strandentwining cable of all flesh. That is why mystic monks.

(James Joyce *Ulysses*)[103]

The portrait of Aaron in the Church of St. Magnus the Martyr invites a brief look at James Joyce's *Ulysses*, particularly the clerical figure mocked by Buck Mulligan on the opening pages. Currently read as representing a modern priest, he is also in significant part Aaron, the first high priest. That Aaron is also present from the onset in *Ulysses* points to an extraordinary conversation between these modernist masterworks.

The first book of this series shows the connection between *The Waste Land* and the imagery of the altarpiece in that church. It explores the relationship between Aaron and his sacred carbuncle gem, the 'young man carbuncular' [231], and the carbuncle eyes of Milton's Satan in *Paradise Lost*. It also reveals how both the church and the poem are linked to the Temple of Solomon through the white and gold colours of the altarpiece in a previous manifestation and the 'white and gold' [265] of the First Temple. In *Ulysses*, each chapter or 'episode' is linked with themes such as a form of art, organs of the body, and a colour scheme. The colours of the opening episode of *Ulysses* in which the mocked priest figure appears are also white and gold: 'Art: theology; Colors: white, gold'.[104]

Eliot recognised *Ulysses* as an instant masterpiece of world literature, and in turn uses it to serve his own poetic masterpiece. He deploys it as a literary source in the manner of his use of the Bible, Dante's *Inferno*, the works of Shakespeare and Milton and many others. These works are also deployed extensively in *Ulysses* and, notably often, it is the same aspect, section, or scene, such as Ariel's song in *The Tempest*, Hamlet act IV.v., and the figure of the ancient Queen of Heaven or 'Mighty Mother' comingled with the Virgin Mary.[105]

A theme central to both *Ulysses* and *The Waste Land* is Hebraism and Hellenism, the core influences Mathew Arnold and others identify as informing Western culture. In Eliot's poem, the concept is represented by the conjoined guides Sappho and Aaron. In *Ulysses*, 'Jewgreek is Greekjew. Extremes meet', an observation made to Stephen Dedalus, and he also conjoins the Classical and Judeo-Christian in poetry and music during his conversation with Kitty. 'The rite is the poet's rest. It may be an old hymn to Demeter or also illustrate *Coela enarrant gloriam Domini*'.[106]

Central to that Jew-Greek construction in both *Ulysses* and *The Waste Land* is the priest figure. In episode one of *Ulysses*, the symbol of which in the Gilbert schema is the 'heir', the traditional priest of religion is reconfigured for a future in which God may be dead. He takes many forms through history and prehistory in *Ulysses*, and terminates in modernity in two identifiable post-religious priests. They are the overman of Nietzsche and the artist-priest of Mallarmé. Both intend to help humanity avoid the abyss of nothingness, of nihilism, opened by the fall of God.

Jewel Spears-Brooker observes that Stéphane Mallarmé, from the group of French poets who influenced Eliot, 'claims that Catholicism, in which certainty and darkness were harmonised beautifully, "has ceased," but the human need that generated Catholicism remains. The "honor" of soldiering the abyss, of enabling people to cope with the fear of the unknown, has been inherited by artists.'[107] It shows the idea of the artist as secular priest-guide to be a theme of modernism, rather than exclusive to Nietzsche and Joyce. Joyce's avatar in the novel, Stephen Dedalus, is one such candidate, who in a form of procession with Bloom as an 'exodus from the house of bondage', holds a 'Diaconal Hat on Ashplant'.[108] In the Church, the diaconate undertakes pastoral and teaching work, and Dedalus's ashplant is the staff of the guides Moses and Aaron that we will see arise elsewhere in primeval form in *Ulysses*. Dedalus as 'heir' is setting forth as the apprentice-priest of culture and guide to the populace of modernity. The roots of such priest are in ancients such as Aaron, who morphs in modernity into the secular guide who reveals existential solace in art. This evolving priest figure of philosophy and literature enters the same 1920s mythopoetic space as Eliot's typist and clerk as a modern Eve and Adam.

From the outset in *Ulysses*, Stephan Dedalus also inhabits the figure of Nietzsche's overman in that aspect of the new priest of the arts who must infill, according to Nietzsche, the space vacated by the now dead God. This is suggested through the Adam of *Ulysses*. 'My twelfth rib is gone, he cried. I'm the *Übermensch*. Toothless Kinch and I, the supermen'. The young men who through mockery reject Rome on the opening pages of *Ulysses* become Joyce's new Adamic overmen of Dublin, as Gifford explains. 'Zarathustra asserts: "The most contemptable thing is *the last man*." Thus, since Mulligan's "twelfth rib is gone", he is Adam, first man, least contemptible man — in other words, superman'.[109] *Ulysses* opens as Mulligan descends a stairs, as does the young man carbuncular of *The Waste Land* [248]. Mulligan mocks the Catholic Mass and the modern priest.

Stately, plump Buck Mulligan came from the stairhead, bearing a bowl of lather on which a mirror and a razor lay crossed. A yellow dressing gown, ungirdled, was sustained gently behind him on the mild morning air. He held a bowl aloft and intoned: — *Introibo ad altare Dei*

At the end of that chapter Mulligan stands erect in Nietzschean prayer. Mirroring the opening page, he now mocks a different creed, the new secular creed of Nietzsche and his fictional prophet Zarathustra. That creed of the will to power inverts traditional concepts of good and evil so that the only good is what is good for a pseudo-aristocratic few. Reflecting that, Mulligan inverts Christian communal morality so that it serves Nietzsche's overman as the lord of that proposed ruling cabal.

Buck Mulligan erect, with joined hands before him, said solemnly:

He who stealeth from the poor lendeth to the Lord
Thus spake Zarathustra.

Despite Buck Mulligan's claims to that status, the narrative and imagery of *Ulysses* suggest that the aspect of Stephen Dedalus which represents Joyce is the true overman, the new high priest of the arts who, through art, will ameliorate the distress of the Nietzschean death of God. Dedalus as Irish overman is a theme in Joyce's work. Robert Spoo notes that Joyce 'in 1904 signed his letters "James Overman" and "Stephen Dedalus" with equal ironic arrogance'. In *Ulysses* there is 'Mead of our fathers for the *Übermensch*'.[110] Joyce and his Dedalus also quickly transcend Nietzsche's fictional character as the proposed new man of the future, finding him a deficient solution. In *Dubliners*, Joyce had already shown the puritan consequences of adhering to Nietzschean dogma in his short story 'A Painful Case'. The overman is also rejected by Eliot, and book one of this series introduced the ruthless critique of Nietzsche's overman as the dark Adam of egoist modernity through the 'young man carbuncular' [231].

The Nietzschean priest of the future is discarded as a zealot puritan cloaked in the language of freedom. What of the first priest of the ancient past? The question to be asked of the opening priest figure in *Ulysses* is whether Joyce would miss or ignore the opportunity to include the Judeo-Christian history and origin of that priest. That is the biblically mandated first high priest Aaron, a fundamental ancient nexus of Hebraism within the 'Jewgreek' of *Ulysses*.

> And thou shalt put upon Aaron the holy garments, and anoint him, and sanctify him; that he may minister unto me in the priest's office. And thou shalt bring his sons, and clothe them with coats: And thou shalt anoint them, as thou didst anoint their father, that they may minister unto me in the priest's office: for their anointing shall surely be an everlasting priesthood throughout their generations.
>
> (Exodus 40:13-15).

In his magnus opus, and understanding his focus on ancient myth and origins, it is compelling to think Joyce would not. As Nietzsche's overman is engaged from episode one, so also is the first priest Aaron, particularly since, in the Joycean schema of that episode, the modern priest is 'heir' to the priesthood of Aaron.

Mulligan's mocking intonation on the opening page, *Introibo ad altare Dei*, 'I will go up to God's altar', is commonly linked to Psalm 43:4 of the Bible. A more detailed ritual approach to God's altar is that of Aaron.

> And Moses said unto Aaron, Go unto the altar, and offer thy sin offering, and thy burnt offering, and make an atonement

for thyself, and for the people: and offer the offering of
the people, and make an atonement for them; as the Lord
commanded.

Aaron therefore went unto the altar, and slew the calf of
the sin offering, which was for himself.

And the sons of Aaron brought the blood unto him:
and he dipped his finger in the blood, and put it upon the
horns of the altar, and poured out the blood at the bottom
of the altar:

But the fat, and the kidneys, and the caul above the liver
of the sin offering, he burnt upon the altar; as the Lord commanded Moses.

(Leviticus 9)

In the Dublin of *Ulysses*, there is a correspondence between the
everyday activities of the central Jewish character Leopold Bloom
and Aaronic Hebrew ritual. As one of the 'wanderers on the earth'
he evokes the Hebrews of Exodus, and he enjoys kidneys. 'Mr. Leopold Bloom ate with relish the inner organs of beasts and fowls.
He liked thick giblet soup, nutty gizzards, a stuffed roast heart, liv-
erslices fried with crustcrumbs, fried hencods' roes. Most of all he
liked grilled mutton kidneys which gave to his palate a fine tang of
faintly scented urine'. In the scheme of *Ulysses*, the symbolic body
organ of episode four is the kidney. 'In ancient Jewish rites, (as in
"the sacrifice and ceremonies of consecrating the priests," Exodus
29:1-28), kidneys were regarded as the "special parts to be burned
upon the altar as a gift to Yahweh"'. When the 'coals were redden-
ing' in Bloom's breakfast fire, they are also the coals of Hebrew
sacrificial altars in the tabernacle in the desert, in the Temple of
Solomon, and in all such places of altar sacrifice. It is unlikely that
Joyce would reach back to the origins of Judeo-Christian ritual in

this way without including Aaron, the original high priest biblically mandated to conduct those rituals.[111]

Buck Mulligan's missing girdle, his razor, and his bowl of lather and mirror are all more directly related to Aaron than a modern priest. Those that do relate to the modern priest are inherited from Aaron, and some can be seen in portrait form on the Magnus Martyr altarpiece. The priest's girdle, evoked through Mulligan's dishabille appearance in his 'yellow dressinggown, ungirdled', is explained further by Gifford: 'When a priest celebrates Mass, the alb, the long white linen robe with tapered sleeves that he wears, is secured by a girdle, a narrow band ending in tassels'. That girdle is originally Aaron's.[112]

> And thou shalt gird them with girdles, Aaron and his sons, and put the bonnets on them: and the priest's office shall be theirs for a perpetual statute: and thou shalt consecrate Aaron and his sons.
>
> (Exodus 29:9)

This is the same chapter of Exodus in which the carbuncle gem is named in Aaron's Breastplate of Judgement, worn in the portrait on the altarpiece in Magnus Martyr. It is also in these sections of Exodus that the duties, rituals, and garments of the High Priest Aaron are stipulated as he goes 'up to God's altar.' Buck is 'bearing a bowl of lather on which a mirror and a razor lay crossed'. The cross is a Christian symbol, but the Jewishness of Jesus, Mary and the apostles is made clear from Mulligan's continued mocking: '*My mother's a jew*'. Mulligan's razor is that of Aaron, since it denotes 'the sign of the slaughterer, the priest as butcher'.[113] Whereas a modern priest never draws ritual blood, Aaron is a slaughterer, evidenced in Leviticus and Exodus.

Then shalt thou kill the ram, and take of his blood, and put
it upon the tip of the right ear of Aaron, and upon the tip
of the right ear of his sons, and upon the thumb of their
right hand, and upon the great toe of their right foot, and
sprinkle the blood upon the altar round about.

(Exodus 29:20)

The remaining elements of Buck's shaving ritual all evoke the pre-
Christian, Hebraic roots of the priest. The 'bowl of lather' echoes
the laver bowl, a large bowl filled with water for cleansing rituals
said to be located outside both the Tabernacle in the desert and the
First Temple.

And the LORD spake unto Moses, saying, Thou shalt also
make a laver of brass, and his foot also of brass, to wash
withal: and thou shalt put it between the tabernacle of
the congregation and the altar, and thou shalt put water
therein. For Aaron and his sons shall wash their hands and
their feet thereat: When they go into the tabernacle of the
congregation, they shall wash with water, that they die not;

(Exodus 30:17-20)

Buck's mirror evokes the mirrors supplied by the women for the
base of that laver. 'And he made the laver of brass, and the foot of
it of brass, of the lookingglasses of the women assembling, which
assembled at the door of the tabernacle of the congregation'
(Exodus 38). The surrender of their mirrors is an Old Testament
metaphor for the mandated abasement of female vanity in the face
of the male God and the Adamic glory of his earthy doppelgänger
man. This scribal condemnation of female vanity continues in
Milton's *Paradise Lost* through Eve's narcissistic contemplation of

her reflection. It becomes a 'watry image' on meeting Adam, since her 'beauty is excelld by manly grace | And wisdom, which alone is truly fair.' Adam details the consequences of her vanity. 'Out of my sight, thou Serpent that name best | Befits thee with him leagu'd, thy self as false | And hateful ... Not to be trusted, longing to be seen | Though by the Devil himself'.[114]

The looking-glass is echoed in *The Waste Land* in the Cleopatra figure's 'glass' [78] and the typist's 'glass' [249], posing the question how women might know themselves in light of the reflection of millennia of male scribal perspectives engendered by the Eve myth. The 'glass' of 1922 was not only a mirror, it was also the monocle. In *Ulysses* the 'bony form' of the pretentiously named Cashel Boyle O'Connor Fitzmaurice Tisdall Farrell 'strode along the curbstone from the river staring with a rapt gaze into the sunlight through a heavystringed glass'.[115] It is also a lens in Eliot's Harvard thesis. In discussing the interplay of identity and memory, he writes of an idea that it 'is not a glass through which we descry a past reality'.[116] In that sense of a lens, the glass of *The Waste Land* includes a one-eyed male perspective and recalls St. Paul: 'For now we see through a glass, darkly; but then face to face: now I know in part; but then shall I know even as also I am known' (1 Corinthians 13). Virginia Woolf sharply observes that the true scribal aim is the inflation of man's reflection.

> Women have served all these centuries as looking-glasses possessing the magic and delicious power of reflecting the figure of man at twice its natural size. Without that power probably the earth would still be swamp and jungle. The glories of all our wars would be unknown. We should still be scratching the outlines of deer on the remains of mutton bones and bartering flints for sheep skins or whatever simple ornament took our unsophisticated taste. Supermen

and Fingers of Destiny would never have existed. The Czar and the Kaiser would never have worn crowns or lost them. Whatever may be their use in civilized societies, mirrors are essential to all violent and heroic action. That is why Napoleon and Mussolini both insist so emphatically upon the inferiority of women, for if they were not inferior, they would cease to enlarge. That serves to explain in part the necessity that women so often are to men. And it serves to explain how restless they are under her criticism; how impossible it is for her to say to them this book is bad, this picture is feeble, or whatever it may be, without giving far more pain and rousing far more anger than a man would do who gave the same criticism. For if she begins to tell the truth, the figure in the looking-glass shrinks; his fitness for life is diminished. How is he to go on giving judgement, civilizing natives, making laws, writing books, dressing up and speechifying at banquets, unless he can see himself at breakfast and at dinner at least twice the size he really is?

(Virginia Woolf *A Room of One's Own* 1928)[117]

Confirming that Joyce had Aaron in mind, Bloom's recapitulation of his various rituals of the day creates links in *Ulysses* with Old Testament rituals, including the 'burnt offering' and the 'Holy of Holies'. There is a reference to Aaron's 'Urim and Thummim', described by Gifford as 'Hebrew: "Light" and "Perfection" or "Fire" and "Truth"; these two symbols, which the priest wears on his Breastplate of Judgement, suggest doctrine and faith, the ever-present possibility of a revelationary perception of God's will'.[118] There is some confusion here, as the Urim and Thummim were not connected to the Breastplate of Judgement. The breastplate is prominent on the Magnus Martyr portrait but neither the Urim nor Thummim are evident, as they were oracular objects kept separately — something even the lauded biblical scholar Milton confuses.

> The Urim and Thummim were part of the high priest's equipment in ancient Israel, kept in a pocket or bag integral to the priestly ephod. They may have been two stones or sticks; they were used in divinatory practices for determining God's will ... In Milton's *Paradise Lost*, when Christ rides out to vanquish the rebel angels, he is armed with "radiant *Urim*, work divinely wrought", symbolic of his role as Judge and Light incarnate. Elsewhere Milton refers to the oracular power of Urim in *Reason of Church Government* and again in *Paradise Regained* to "the Oracle / *Urim* and *Thummim*, those oraculous gems / on *Aaron's* breast."[119]

To return to the razor as 'the sign of the slaughterer, the priest as butcher'.[120] It is a running theme in *Ulysses*, including in the figurative human sacrifice of the Irish nationalist Robert Emmet. There are traces here of the oldest of rituals, including that of the yearly bloodletting or human sacrifice of Eliot's 'Hanged Man' [55], explored in the next essay. Apart from the Christ imagery, the method of death, the instruments, the executioner as a form of priest, the slaughter of lambs and the vessels to collect the viscera and blood all echo Old Testament rituals. 'Moses took half of the blood and put it in basins, and the other half of the blood he sprinkled on the altar' (Exodus 24:6) and, 'without shedding of blood there is no forgiveness' (Hebrews 9:22). There seems a suggestion that the priest figure can quickly mutate into something more sinister.

> The learned prelate who administered the last comforts of holy religion to the hero martyr when about to pay the death

penalty knelt in a most christian spirit in a pool of rainwater, his cassock above his hoary head, and offered up to the throne of grace fervent prayers of supplication. Hand by the block stood the grim figure of the executioner, his visage being concealed in a tengallon pot with two circular perforated apertures through which his eyes glowered furiously. As he awaited the fatal signal he tested the edge of his horrible weapon by honing it upon his brawny forearm or decapitated in rapid succession a flock of sheep which had been provided by the admirers of his fell but necessary office. On a handsome mahogany table near him were neatly arranged the quartering knife, the various finely tempered disembowelling appliances (specially supplied by the worldfamous firm of cutlers, Messrs John Round and Sons, Sheffield), a terra cotta saucepan for the reception of the duodenum, colon, blind intestine and appendix etc when successfully extracted and two commodious milkjugs destined to receive the most precious blood of the most precious victim.[121]

The priest figure as a continuum from ancient sources in the novel is not limited to the classical Mediterranean or the Judeo-Christian. There is also the druid, introduced in the opening chapter when Buck Mulligan, pleased to have secured a loan from Stephan, declares they will 'have a glorious drunk to astonish the druidy druids'. By episode eight the druid shows Old Testament behaviours when Leopold Bloom is handed a religious leaflet on the street, sparking a stream of thought. 'His slow feet walked him riverward, reading. Are you saved? All are washed in the blood of the lamb. God wants blood victim. Birth, hymen, martyr, war, foundation of a building, sacrifice, kidney burntoffering, druid's altars'.[122] The druid closes episode nine as the 'druid priests of Cymbeline', linking the time of Shakespeare's Britian to the Britannia of the Romans and its more ancient Celtic past. By episode twelve, *Cyclops* — the symbolic organ being the muscle, the symbol the Fenian and the technique 'gigantism' — that ancient past gives rise to an extraordinary figure, the palaeolithic Celtic Ur-priest of *Ulysses*.

The figure seated on a large boulder at the foot of a round tower was that of a broadshouldered deepchested stronglimbed frankeyed redhaired freely freckled shaggy bearded widemouthed largenosed longheaded deepvoiced barekneed brawnyhanded hairylegged ruddyfaced, sinewyarmed hero. From shoulder to shoulder he measured several ells and his rocklike mountainous knees were covered, as was likewise the rest of his body wherever visible, with a strong growth of tawny prickly hair in hue and toughness similar to the mountain gorse (Ulex Europeus). The widewinged nostrils, from which bristles of the same tawny hue piojected, were of such capaciousness that within their cavernous obscurity the fieldlark might easily have lodged her nest. The eyes in which a tear and a smile strove ever for the mastery were of the dimensions of a goodsized cauliflower. A powerful current of warm breath issued at regular intervals from the profound cavity of his mouth while in rhythmic resonance the loud strong hale reverberations of his formidable heart thundered rumblingly causing the ground, the summit of the lofty tower and the still loftier walls of the cave to vibrate and tremble.

He wore a long unsleeved garment of recently flayed oxhide reaching to the knees in a loose kilt and this was bound about his middle by a girdle of plaited straw and rushes ... From his girdle hung a row of seastones which jangled at every movement of his portentous frame and on these were graven with rude yet striking art the tribal images of many Irish heroes and heroines of antiquity ... A couched spear of acuminated granite rested by him while at his feet reposed a savage animal of the canine tribe whose stertorous gasps announced that he was sunk in uneasy slumber, a supposition confirmed by hoarse growls and spasmodic movements which his master repressed from time to time by tranquilising blows of a mighty cudgel rudely fashioned out of paleolithic stone.[123]

This first priest of Ireland (whose hound may be the Celtic Bran) is also the Ur-hero, written in a form of exaggeration that is likely to have inflected the mythmakers of ancient times as they lauded their tribal leaders, the source of their livelihood. He wears graven images, as does Aaron in the carved gems on his Breastplate of Judgement, images that include human archetypes also present in *The Waste Land*, such as Cleopatra, the Buddha, and Adam and Eve. His palaeolithic cudgel is the staff of Moses and Aaron, as is Dedalus's ashplant. The long unsleeved garment reaching the knee and bound about his middle by a girdle are the Ephod and girdle of Aaron described in Exodus 28, which became the Alb and girdle of the modern priest. Similarly, his 'row of seastones which jangled at every movement' echo Aaron's row of pomegranates and bells that encircle the bottom of his garments so that he does not surprise the Lord. 'A golden bell and a pomegranate, a golden bell and a pomegranate, upon the hem of the robe round about. And it shall be upon Aaron to minister: and his sound shall be heard when he goeth in unto the holy place before the Lord, and when he cometh out, that he die not' (Exodus 28:34).

This paleo-priest seems to be Joyce's representation of the true first priest, long before the time of Aaron. He is another of the many origin stories in *Ulysses*, the rise of the priest figure throughout ancient cultures. He is the figurative palaeolithic template for Aaron as Aaron is the template for the modern priest. 'The cords of all link back, strandentwining cable of all flesh. That is why mystic monks'.

The figures of the ancient and modern priest, the druid and the overman are the recurring companions of Dedalus and Bloom in *Ulysses*, and that includes the figure of the first high priest Aaron. Since in *The Waste Land* Aaron is linked with the carbuncular clerk as street overman through the carbuncle gem, three inferences might be drawn. Eliot would have understood the allusions to Aaron on the opening pages of *Ulysses*. Sitting in Magnus Martyr, he could not have failed to connect *Ulysses* thematically to the portrait in that church. And, since there are many other resonances, shared themes and motifs, and shared specific references, Eliot has inbuilt into *The Waste Land* a deliberate, significant conversation with *Ulysses*.

9. The Voyage to Kythira

Baudelaire's Cadaverous Jesus and The Hanged Man

> I do not find
> The Hanged Man. Fear death by water.
>
> (*The Waste Land* 54-5)

The 'Hanged Man' [55] is a representation of the yearly dying god who exists in many forms in myth and in *The Waste Land*. Such hanging refers not to death by rope, but to being tied or fixed to a tree or wooden construction. In ancient ritual, that man was sometimes representational, shaped from vegetation or wood. In other instances, he was a priest, initiate or unlucky chosen one who represents the god, and his fate ranged from token bloodletting into the soil to ritual death. A significant purpose of the ritual of the hanged man in ancient times was to engender new growth in the spring.

The Roman crucifixion was later coopted into that religious symbolism, in which form the Hanged Man is the Christian Christ. That he is in part the Hanged Man of the poem is suggested in the capitalisation of that title, through such imagery as Eastertime, and in the relationship between the 'violet hour' [215] and the violet covers over imagery in the Church of St. Magnus the Martyr during Easter as a sign of mourning for the dead Christ.[124] In *The Golden Bough*, Frazer notes the strong similarities between Christ and the dying god Attis whose yearly death, like many of the dying gods, was in some form a hanged man and whose blood was said to be coloured violet. We will see Charles Baudelaire's carrion birds feast on the rotting corpse of the hanged god shortly.

The power of this myth was not lost on Nietzsche. On the one hand, he ends his autobiography with '*Dionysos against the crucified*', his mantra of antagonism to a society informed by Christian morality. On the other, not one to allow spiritual imagery to exist without co-opting it, he uses that imagery to signify the suffering of his avatar, the philosophical fictional prophet Zarathustra, as he attempts to engender the reformation that prepares the way for his overman.

> They'll certainly "dissolve" you,
> They no doubt hunger after your "dissolution,"
> Indeed they flutter about you, their enigma,
> Around you, hanged man! ...
> Oh Zarathustra! ...
> Self-knower! ...
> Self-hangman! ...
>   (Nietzsche *Amid Birds of Prey* 1888)[125]

Underlying the dying gods Adonis, Attis and Osiris of Eliot's Notes, Dionysus was so close to Osiris that they were merged into the Greco-Egyptian syncretic deity Dionysus-Osiris, as there was an Isis-Aphrodite. Harrison and Eliot see Dionysus as an early expression of the dying god of which Christ is the later Christian manifestation. Since Harrison writes that 'Dionysos is not only the beautiful young wine-god, but also an ancient tree-god', his genesis is in animism, the 'vegetation ceremonies' of the preamble to the Notes.[126]

This crossover point between the ancient and modern dying god is also seen, in dark form, in Baudelaire's *Un Voyage a Cythere*, 'A Voyage to Cythera'. Kythera, one of the Ionian Islands, is the birthplace of Aphrodite and her Roman equivalent Venus, the Greek and Roman goddesses of love. According to Homer, Aphrodite is crowned with violets. 'I will sing of stately Aphrodite, gold-crowned and beautiful ... they brought her to the gods, who welcomed her when they saw her, giving her their hands. Each one of them prayed that he might lead her home to be his wedded wife, so greatly were they amazed at the beauty of violet-crowned Cytherea.'[127] In 1910 Eliot wrote a poem of similar title and subject, *Embarquement pour Cythère*, inspired both by Baudelaire and the original painting.

Eliot's own writing reveals his interest in Old Master pictures as well as his propensity to poke fun at them. Decades before visiting the museum, he experimented with ekphrasis — the practice of describing an artwork in detail — in poems such as "Embarquement pour Cythère" (1910), which lampoons the courtly pleasure-seekers embarking for the island of Venus's birth in Jean-Antoine Watteau's 1717 painting of the same name ... Though Eliot repudiated the bourgeois fetishization of the Old Masters, he was highly literate in the Western canon.[128]

L'embarquement pour Cythère is a 1717 rococo painting by Jean-Antoine Watteau, created during the reign of the sun-king Louis XIV. Watteau's painting 'became Baudelaire's *Un Voyage a Cythere*' of 1857, and Eliot 'quoted 'well-known lines from it in *Baudelaire in Our Time*', his essay of 1927.[129] The title of the painting is translated variously as the Embarkation for Cythera, Voyage to Cythera and Pilgrimage to Cythera. It depicts a group of people engaged in a fête galante, a courtship party, a term coined to describe the event in the painting. It is in turn derived from the fête champêtre, the party of the field, the costume parties held in the gardens of the palace of Versailles enacting scenes of pastoral simplicity, often including aspects of myth and folk tale.

The fête galante of *L'embarquement pour Cythère* portrays a pilgrimage to the classical goddess of love so that she might favour the pilgrims by binding them with partners or lovers. In contrast to the *Night Vigil of Venus* [428n], both the fête champêtre and the fête galante were lightweight affairs of no significant spiritual import.[130] However the voyage itself, when transposed into poetry by Baudelaire, Eliot and Hope Mirrlees, becomes significant.

> Le Départ pour Cythére
>
> These Nymphs are harmless,
> Fear not their soft mouths —
> Some Pasteur made the Gauls immune
> Against the bite of Nymphs ... look
> (Hope Mirrlees *Paris: A Poem* 1920)

Eliot's poem *Embarquement pour Cythère* shows an early interest in that intersection of modernity with degraded myth. It features Sappho's evening star, a fundamental mythic representation of female divinity throughout the ancient Mediterranean, including Aphrodite, and resonates with the degraded votive offerings later suggested by the 'cigarette ends' [188] of *The Waste Land*.

> (As long as a cigarette will burn
> When you light it at the evening star)
> (*Embarquement pour Cythère* 11-12)[131]

An over-costumed society voided of mythic, spiritual and cultural depth seems the target of Eliot's poem, ending as it does with the denizens imbibing their philosophy 'through a paper straw!'. Such shallowness is also the target of Baudelaire. Among the resonances,

there is in Baudelaire's poem a striking, cadaverous version of the
'Hanged Man' [55] of *The Waste Land*.

"What is that sad dark island?" "It's renowned
and legendary — known as Cythera.
For old-time people it's Utopia.
Despite all that, it seems a wretched land."

— Island of feasting hearts and hidden joys,
like an aroma the licentious ghost
of Aphrodite flies around your coast,
Inflaming souls with love and listlessness.
...
She wasn't there but, as we grazed the shore
and our bright canvas scared the gulls away,
we saw a triple-forking gallows tree,
black as a cypress, sticking in the air.

Ferocious birds were perched on what they ate —
a savaged, overripe and hanged cadaver.
Each of them used his foul beak like a lever
To pry out every little bit of rot.

The eyes were pits, and the intestines hung
the whole way from the belly to the thighs.
The birds went also for the delicacies —
They ripper the private parts out of the thing.

There were four-footed creatures. Eager maws
lifted, they padded round and round the feast,
Dead center of them moved the largest beast,

an executioner with his deputies.
...
Ridiculous hanged man, your grief is mine.
While looking at you hanging on display,
I felt rise to my teeth, like nausea,
a stream of bile, a flood of ancient pain.
...
O Venus, on your isle, I only found
a gallows where my form was hanging — me!
Lord, grant me strength enough to see,
without revulsion, my own body and mind!

(Baudelaire *Un Voyage a Cythere*)[132]

Baudelaire's bleak imagery imagines the scene of the yearly death
of the dying god who is more ancient than Christ, as he is in *The
Waste Land*. The scent and sight of carnal decay is also the scent of
the death of myth and, as Nietzsche later points out, the death of
all gods at the hands of science. That in in turn illuminates Mirrlees
poem: some 'Pasteur made the Gauls immune | Against the bite of
Nymphs'. Elsewhere we met Baudelaire's Satan, and he seems again
present in beast form at this scene of the death of God as 'the larg-
est beast | an executioner with his deputies'.[133] In Baudelaire's poetic
inhabitation of the figure of that hanged man there is intense tor-
ment, personal and spiritual, expressed in a way more pagan than
Christian through the ancient relationship between the hanged
man figure and the 'ghost of ancient Aphrodite', whose loss to the
world he laments. The relationship on Baudelaire's island reflects
that of the Adonis, Attis and Osiris of Eliot's Notes through their
relationships to Aphrodite, Cybele and Isis.

In 1927 Eliot wrote of Baudelaire that it 'is now becoming
understood that Baudelaire is one of the few poets who wrote

nothing, either prose or verse that is negligible. To understand Baudelaire you must read the whole of Baudelaire. And nothing that he wrote is without importance. He was a great poet; he was a great critic. And he was also a man with a profound attitude toward life, for the study of which we need every scrap of his writing.'[134] Since by that time Eliot was about to formally commit to the Anglo-Catholic creed, at first sight this seems an extraordinary esteem in view of Baudelaire's famed Satanism. His understanding and admiration of Baudelaire shows that Eliot's perspective on a spiritual life goes beyond the simplified Manichean dogmas of Christian creeds. He does not abandon such persons. He visits with them their dark places, even considering them more spiritually alive than the Dantesque dead souls trudging over London Bridge [62].

> It was once the mode to take Baudelaire's Satanism seriously, as it is now the tendency to present Baudelaire as a serious and Catholic Christian. Especially as a prelude to the *Journaux Intimes* this diversity of opinion needs some discussion. I think that the latter view — that Baudelaire is essentially Christian — is nearer the truth than the former, but it needs considerable reservation. When Baudelaire's Satanism is dissociated from its less creditable paraphernalia, it amounts to a dim intuition of a part, but a very important part, of Christianity. Satanism itself, so far as not merely an affectation, was an attempt to get into Christianity by the back door. Genuine blasphemy, genuine in spirit and not purely verbal, is the product of partial belief, and is as impossible to the complete atheist as to the perfect Christian. It is a way of affirming belief. This state of partial belief is manifest throughout the *Journaux Intimes*. What is significant about Baudelaire is his theological innocence. He is discovering

Christianity for himself; he is not assuming it as a fashion or weighing social or political reasons, or any other accidents. He is beginning, in a way, at the beginning; and being a discoverer, is not altogether certain what he is exploring and to what it leads; he might almost be said to be making again, as one man, the effort of scores of generations.[135]

Eliot wrote these observations in 1930, by then formally committed to Anglo-Catholicism. It shows his understanding of spirituality to be complex, distinct from religious cliché. The intricately wrought scaffolding of his commitment to this creed was in significant part constructed in the act of writing *The Waste Land*, in which Baudelaire plays a significant role. The idea that Baudelaire accesses what Eliot describes as a 'rudimentary or embryonic' Christianity through the 'back door' of Satanism yields insight into that scaffolding. For Eliot, spirituality and culture are entwined, and spiritual quest is often expressed in the imagery of culture. That is so even in the darkest imagery, such as that of Baudelaire, and even if the artist is not fully aware of their own quest.

'The important fact about Baudelaire is that he was essentially a Christian, born out of his due time, and a classicist, born out of his due time ... Baudelaire was not an aesthetic or a political Christian; his tendency to "ritual" ... springs from no attachment to the outward forms of Christianity, but from the instincts of a soul that was *naturaliter* Christian'. Eliot's *naturaliter* Christian is the *Anima Naturaliter Christiana*, the 'natural Christian soul' proposed by those such as the early Church father Tertullian. That understanding accepts the metaphysical authenticity of the 'virtuous pagan'.[136] The idea is applied to the poet Virgil as he guides Dante through the underworld. It informs the continuums of *The Waste Land*, in which all sincere efforts to commune with what is in essence one godhead are not to be doubted as sincere spiritual quest. It is, or at least was an aspect of the universal church theology of Anglo-Catholicism, evident in the comment of John Henry Newman in 1833. 'Do you then unchurch all the Presbyterians ... Nay, we are not judging others ... we do not therefore exclude either from salvation. ... Neither do we desire to pass sentence on other persons of other countries ... because similar difficulties may be raised about virtuous Heathens, Jews, or Mahometans.'[137]

Eliot wrote in 1921 that all 'first-rate poetry is occupied with morality: this is the lesson of Baudelaire. More than any poet of his time, Baudelaire was aware of what most mattered: the problem of good and evil.'[138] In the first book of this series we saw that Baudelaire's Satan is brought to *The Waste Land* from the outset, and it is clear that it is that entire book of poems that is important. What Eliot sees in *The Flowers of Evil* is a spiritual spectrum, a map of Baudelaire's spiritual journey from 'hermit of the brothel' to a version of the Christian, however dark and embryonic, in his hanged man. The hanged man of Cythera is a totemistic poetic milestone on that quest. That represents a remarkable and agonised change, since we saw he was initially equally committed, like St. Augustine, to his youthful dissolute life. It informs the struggle and difficulty deliberately inbuilt in the quest and pilgrimage themes of *The Waste Land*.

Eliot's interest in Baudelaire resonates with other themes of *The Waste Land*. There is the emergence from the brute to the cultured and spiritual in Baudelaire's life and poetry: 'in the adjustment of the natural to the spiritual, of the bestial to the human and the human to the supernatural, Baudelaire is a bungler compared with Dante; the best that can be said, and that is a very great deal, is that what he knew he found out for himself'. It is a bestiality that Eliot's pustular clerk will never throw off, inured as he is by the self-aggrandising philosophies of egoism. Eliot closes his essay with the comment that 'Baudelaire came to attain the greatest, the most difficult, of the Christian virtues, the virtue of humility. Only by long and devoted study of the man and his work and his life can we appreciate the significance of that great passage in *Mon Coeur Mis à Nu*.

To pray every morning to God, the source of all power and all justice; to my father, to Mariette and to Poe, as intercessors; that they may give me the necessary strength to fulfil all my appointed tasks and that they may grant my mother a sufficient span of life in which to enjoy my transformation; to work all day long, or as long, at any rate, as my strength allows me; to put my trust in God, that is, in Justice itself, for the success of my plans; to offer, every evening, a further prayer, asking God for life and strength for my mother and myself; to divide all my earnings into four parts — one for current expenses, one for my creditors, one for my friends and one for my mother — to obey the strictest principles of sobriety, the first being abstinence from all stimulants whatsoever.[139]

The facts of Baudelaire's late life may not have wholly matched his intentions. He remained an addict and a drinker, and his mother sent him money. He was always attached to his mother and hated his stepfather, whereas Nietzsche deeply grieved the loss of his father and subsequently began to hate his mother, sister and the other women in his familial home. Both had a problematic relationship with modernity. Whereas Nietzsche's reaction is withdrawal from society and polemical insistence on a reformation that facilitates ruthless governance by an pseudo-aristocratic few, Baudelaire and Eliot engage through art with modernity in all its horrors and tensions.

Baudelaire also lived it, and here there is another contrast with Nietzsche. Nietzsche's idealised engagement with life is through the Dionysian, the anarchic aspect of humanity expressed in antiquity in dance, drinking, wild poetry and other means of discarding the ordered, constrained self. Yet he was himself of puritan lifestyle, a rigorously ordered man in behaviour and diet who rarely if ever danced or drank, and may have remained an unwilling virgin. Whereas Baudelaire immersed himself intensely in the Dionysian, for much of his life resisting all efforts, including his own conscience, to curtail his dissolution. He seemed to seek to prove through action what his near contemporary Nietzsche claimed to prove through writing: that morals lack a firm foundation and so can be discarded. As the progress from his Satan to his Christ shows, Baudelaire failed in that, finding the Dionysian wanting.

That evolution, and its extraordinary literary expression, is a significant reason for Baudelaire's presence in *The Waste Land*. Even if that evolution is of a dedicatedly dissolute man coming from an immensely dark place of the soul, it is preferable to Dante's dead souls trudging across London Bridge towards the promises of Mammon in the City of London. The struggle itself is important. Through agonised quest Baudelaire arrived at the spiritual, a remarkable turnaround for the hermit of the brothel. Baudelaire's commitment to change is preceded by others, part of a series of aphorisms with such titles as *Hygiene. Conduct. Method* and *Hygiene. Morality. Conduct.* He urges himself to always 'be a poet, even in prose'; he commits 'to do one's duty every day and trust in God for the morrow'; and asks of himself, 'My phase of egoism, — Is it passed?'.[140]

10. The Ego, the I Pronoun, and the Empress

From Proto-Indo-European to Lithuanian and Modernity

The Proto-Indo-European opening of the poem can be revisited to explore a specific aspect; the primeval emergence of the ego and its representation in the I pronoun. An article of 1934 titled *The Origin of Pronouns of the First and Second Person* yields a glimpse of early twentieth century thinking on personal pronouns, opening with the observation that there 'was in all probability a period in the primitive development of languages when there were no personal pronouns'.[141] In the previous century, an article of 1872 stated that there must 'once have been a period in the history of language when such a thing as a pronoun did not exist'.[142] In literature, in the more poetic language of an essay fundamental to the modernist mythic method Eliot advocated so strongly at the time, W.B. Yeats sketches the amorphous world of the primeval group and the lack of individualist differentiation. 'Men who lived in a world where anything might flow and change, and become any other thing; and among great gods whose passions were in the flaming sunset, and in the thunder and the thunder-shower, had not our thoughts of weight and measure'.[143]

The evolution of pronouns is mapped in the opening verse paragraph of Eliot's poem as a representation of the evolution of the human ego from the communal primeval group of the opening lines to the isolated 'I' of modernity. The linguistic development of pronouns represents the journey of human individualism from its genesis. Laurence Rainey examines this aspect of the poem in granular detail. He notes a progression from the communal 'us' to the plural 'we' to the isolated 'I': 'eight uses of first-person pronouns. The result is slightly staggering.'[144] Rainey reads a 'self-cancelling' result as part of a fragmentation reading of the poem. An alternative reading is that this stepped poetic evolution of pronouns over those opening eighteen lines of poetry represents a progressive continuum from ancient group consciousness to (from certain points of view) an emblematic high point of modern civilisation, the Hapsburg dynasty of the Holy Roman Empire. Within that dynasty, at the close of the nineteenth century there was the tragic story of Empress Elizabeth, who we meet shortly.

'Bin gar keine Russin, stamm' aus Litauen, echt deutsch.'   [12]

Translated as 'Not a Russian, I'm from Lithuania, genuinely German', there has long been an acknowledged dissonance between the claim of the 'Hofgarten' [10] speaker — most often said to be the overheard comment of a stranger — to be both Lithuanian and German.[145] Notwithstanding the politics of the time, a person could not exclusively be both Lithuanian and German.

If the 'speaker' in the poem is not an individual in the Hofgarten but the 'I' itself, the English first person pronoun, that dissonance between Lithuanian and German disappears. The Proto-Indo-European *egóH became the Proto-Germanic *ek from which the Old English ic emerged, later shortened to the modern I. A similar path saw *egóH give rise to the first-person pronouns of Latin and Greek, ego and egó, and the Lithuanian aš. Since in the 1920s such reconstruction was derived from Lithuanian — believed to hold the most faithfully preserved Proto-Indo-European roots — the speaker as 'I' is both originally from — 'aus' — Lithuanian, and genuinely — 'echt' — German, sharing the common root *egóH.[146] The extreme egoisms of modernity that are mythopoetically challenged in *The Waste Land* in the form of the 'young man carbuncular' [231], such as those of Max Stirner and Friedrich Nietzsche, start here, at the genesis of the human ego and the I pronoun.

Two aspects of the translation of that line are notable. First, though 'stamm' aus Litauen' is commonly translated as 'I'm from Lithuania', the German nominative first person pronoun *Ich* — I — as the subject of the line is absent. Second, 'deutsch' is not capitalised, discriminating it from the capitalised 'Russin' and 'Litauen' of the same line. Uncapitalised, *deutsch* directs the reader to its lower-case equivalent in English, the archaic uncapitalised word 'german'. As an adjective, german was used in the archaic hyphenated phrases sister-german and brother-german, meaning 'having the same mother and father', and not to be confused with the proper noun German. It is derived from Middle English *germain*, of Old French origin, in turn derived from Latin *germānus* and *germen*, with meanings such as 'seed', 'offshoot', 'bud' and 'sprout'. It is closely related to the word germane, also from Latin *germānus*, meaning closely or significantly related. The Proto-Indo-European root is $*g'enh_1$- (later becoming $*gen\partial$-), meaning to give birth or to beget, giving rise to such words as genesis, gender, genealogy, genetics, genius and degenerate.

To this can be added the meanings encased in 'stamm'. One translation is 'tribe', returning to our group of primeval humans we have seen open the poem, 'dancing about the darkling rim of the tribal fire-circle'. A closely related German word is *stammin*, meaning a tree trunk, evoking the Proto-Indo-European evolution of language into many daughter languages that mirrors the Darwinian tree of life. Stamm is also a 'stem'. In that way, reflecting the primal growth motif of the opening — the tree of culture that branches throughout the poem — both 'stamm'' and 'deutsch', direct the reader to the words stem, seed and offshoot as linguistic factors in the development of the I pronoun from the Proto-Indo-European *egóH*, the root of the missing *Ich* of the twelfth line of the poem.

Echoing the many maps and continuums of the poem, it continues the theme of the evolution of human languages and cultures. A beneficial evolution of humankind does not necessarily keep pace, since the evolution of the I pronoun arrives at two modern termini in the poem. The first is the pustular clerk of Part III, the man engendered by millennia of vainglorious scribal egoism who, as the dark Adam of modernity, assaults the typist.[147] An earlier terminus in the poem is reached at the end of the first verse paragraph, in the form of the Hapsburg dynasty and Empress Elizabeth, known as 'Sisi.'

A legendary beauty of great personal discipline and poise, she was the wife of Emperor Franz Joseph I, and the adored subject of Countess Marie Louise Larisch's book *My Past*. In Valerie Eliot's book of the drafts of *The Waste Land* there is a note that Eliot had met the countess. 'The assumption was that Eliot must have read the book, but in fact he had met the author (when and where is not known), and his description of the sledding, for example, was taken verbatim from a conversation with this niece and confident of the Austrian Empress Elizabeth.'[148] He is likely to have read Larisch's book, a remarkable account of high dramas at the Hapsburg court. Although it may be the Countess Larisch who is 'frightened' [15] in *The Waste Land*, it is the noted insomniac Empress Elizabeth who was known to 'read, much of the night', and who fled the strictures of the Hapsburg Court to go 'south in the winter' [18] to the grand classical villa she had built on Corfu as a refuge, named the *Achilleion*. She called it 'my sanctuary, where I may belong to me.'[149]

For the sake of focus, and because of its significance, an examination of the full political and social import of the Hapsburg dynasty in the poem is deferred. As a précis, it is entwined with such themes as empire, the rise of Russian communism, and the near-anarchy

and potential collapse of Europe, themes also reflected in Hermann Hesse's essay *Blick in Chaos* [366-76n], 'In Sight of Chaos'.[150]
Empress Elizabeth also informs the theme of the human cultural
continuum, in the form of European cultural interconnectedness.
In *My Past* she meets Wagner [31, 42, 276] and her relative 'Queen
Victoria' [258]. Fundamental and sorrowful aspects of Elizabeth's
life were her alienation within the strictures of the Habsburg court,
her struggles against that, her intense personal isolation because of
that, the death of her son in a murder-suicide, and her eventual assas-
sination as the random victim of anarchist *attentat*, the 'propaganda
of the deed'. Here, we explore the mythic aspect of her presence.

The speaker's rendezvous with the Marie of the poem (and Eliot's
likely rendezvous with Countess Marie Larisch) is in Munich's 'Hof-
garten' [10], the 'court garden' located between the royal palace and
the Englischer Garten, the English Garden. The eight paths of the
Hofgarten all radiate from the Dianatempel, the pavilion of Diana.
She is the goddess who opens James Frazer's *The Golden Bough* of
Eliot's Notes, and is the Roman manifestation of the Greek Artemis.
The Countess Larisch wrote of Empress Elizabeth that 'I looked
upon Elizabeth as being from the old world of the Gods. She was
Artemis — cold, beautiful, arrogant ... her ivory loveliness gleam-
ing in the moonlight when she bathed, like Venus — and in those
scented solicitudes she was like a Pagan called back from the Past ...
Her real place was with the immortals.'[151] We have seen that Venus,
in the form of Sappho's Aphrodite, opens the poem in 'April', and we
have met Artemis with the panpipes of 'Lilacs', the mythic genesis of
music from Pan's lustful pursuit of the nymph Syrinx.

As a cultural figure Elizabeth resonates with the elevated
women of the poem, and with the theme of intense female alienation in a world controlled by men. Through her, the modern aspect
of the pronoun evolution that opens *The Waste Land* also suggests

a potential degeneration. Through the isolated 'I', the map of the development and accentuation of the modern ego through personal pronouns also shows the alienating cost of the cult of the individual for even the most elevated women within modernity.

This examination of the genesis of the I pronoun resonates with an important aspect of what was new in the work of Sappho at the genesis of written literature, suggesting that a different path is available to the human ego. Her poetry is among the first, and certainly the most notable, to adopt the lyric 'I' pronoun, so placing the individual at the centre of the poetry. It seems that, in *The Waste Land*, she stands for a classical genesis of the individual that contrasts to the Lutheran individual from whom the cult of the hero and anti-hero was developed through Milton, Byron and the Romantics, and on to Emerson, Stirner and Nietzsche. Since the young man carbuncular embodies that lineage, the map of the development of the primeval ego into modernity that opens the poem terminates in Part III in that degenerate egotist. In contrast, in Eliot's view Sappho represents a healthy egoism, a more inclusive and communal individualism realised within Classicism. In her case, it is guided by a relationship with the sacred, that being her muse and ally in love Aphrodite, of 'April'. In contrast again, it is from within the iconoclastic, vainglorious male lineage that leads to the pustular clerk that the zealot scribes emerged who destroyed the work of Sappho, leaving only fragments.

What Eliot seems to be creating in the stepped progression of pronouns in the opening of his poem is a representation of the philosophical idea that, as the ego becomes more pronounced, alienation also inevitably becomes more pronounced. That alienation is compounded, for the women of *The Waste Land* such as the typist and Empress Elizabeth, by misogyny. Sigmund Freud wrote of the intense pain caused to the individual ego by the necessary curtailments of society in *Civilisation and its Discontents*, in which the ego both needs that society, and hates it for its chastening strictures. Before that, Schopenhauer wrote of the evolution of humankind that, 'as knowledge attains to distinctness and as consciousness intensifies, there is a proportionate increase in pain, which accordingly reaches its highest degree in man'.[152] This is his *principium individuationis*, what Nietzsche later describes, in his extraordinary phrase in *The Birth of Tragedy*, as the 'wretched bell jar of individuality'.

For Nietzsche, a temporary escape from that wretched bell jar of individuality is achieved in music. He terms it a return to the 'pastoral metaphysical dance', a transcendence also suggested by Eliot in the 'music upon the waters' of the Thames [257]. One aspect is the sound of vespers from the Church of St. Magnus the Martyr, the modern communal ritual the connects, through Sappho, to the most ancient.

11. DA: To Share, and Self-Control

DA

Datta: what have we given?

...

DA

Dayadhvam: I have heard the key

...

DA

Damyata: The boat responded

(*The Waste Land* 400-418]

We have met the primeval fireside group of the opening of *The Waste Land*, heard humanities primal beats in the rhythm of walking and the strike of their axes, and witnessed their dance. Here we look at another ancient utterance, since the poem closes with the repetitive incantation 'DA'. It is at least in part a representation of the Proto-Indo-European $*deh_2$, meaning both to share and to divide, $*deh_2$- eventually becoming $*d\bar{a}$-. It may represent the choice in the poem between community and divisive egoism, which existed in embryonic form in the earliest humans. Since it is 'the thunder' [399] that speaks, it seems again a return to the most basic, amorphous spirituality of humanity, the spiritualism of animism that infuses all that exists.

Those aspects will be explored briefly here with some caveats. An expert in both Proto-Indo-European and Sanskrit should be able to advise to what extent the Sanskrit words derived from that

Proto-Indo-European root modify the original meaning. A further question is the understanding of *dā- in the 1920s: was it as it is today? These and other nuances mean that this essay is early-stage research. That said, the idea that 'DA' encases an Indo-European aspect has critical precedent in Hugh Kenner.

> By 1788 the resemblances among Sanskrit, Greek and Latin had suggested to Sir William Jones the common source we now call Indo-European, to which is ascribed for instance the root lexicographers call *DA. In *The Waste Land*, whose author was less than ten years out of a Sanskrit classroom, DA is the voice of the god in Bridhadaranyaka Upanishad speaking trice out of thunder ... DA becomes *Datta*, give, *Dayadhvam*, sympathise, *Damyata*, control; an etymology which makes sympathy and control not a sentiment and an inference but forms of giving. Primitive wisdom; and we can sense how *Datta* of the heavenly injunction has unravelled from language to language, culture to culture ...[153]

There seems to be many maps in *The Waste Land*, including the development of poetry, a language tree mirroring the Darwinian tree of life, the evolution of the ego, a likely map of philosophy, and others. In that sense, there is no dogma: the multiple evolutions that rise from the multiple geneses in the poem are celebrated. That includes, as one example, the beauty and power of the evolving English language, embedded in the fabric of the poem itself, as a daughter language on the Germanic branch of the Proto-Indo-European language tree.

> THE distinctive feature of the science of language as conceived nowadays is its historical character: a language

or a word is no longer taken as something given once for all, but as a result of previous development and at the same time as the starting-point for subsequent development. This manner of viewing languages constitutes a decisive improvement on the way in which languages were dealt with in previous centuries, and it suffices to mention such words as 'evolution' and 'Darwinism' to show that linguistic research has in this respect been in full accordance with tendencies observed in many other branches of scientific work during the last hundred years.

(Otto Jespersen's *Language,*
Its Nature, Development and Origin 1921)[154]

Eliot's attention to the evolution of English is not only an enjoyment of its current capabilities. He also intends to be an agent of such evolution. In his view, 'poets in our civilization, as it exists at present, must be difficult ... The poet must become more and more comprehensive, more allusive, more indirect, in order to force, to dislocate if necessary, language into his meaning'.[155] Nor are his efforts to reimagine the rhythms of primeval humanity a form of poetic safari, viewed from the removed comfort of the modernist vehicle. For Eliot, the work of the past is present and alive. Through the work of the artist, the past is 'altered by the present as much as the present is directed by the past. And the poet who is aware of this will be aware of great difficulties and responsibilities ... he is not likely to know what is to be done unless he lives in what is not merely the present, but the present moment of the past, unless he is conscious, not of what is dead, but what is already living'.[156] The peoples of history and prehistory in Eliot's poem engage in a conversation with modernity in a way that changes our understanding of each culture, past and present. Part of that is a conversation about language itself.

To pass on to posterity one's own language, more highly
developed, more refined, and more precise than it was
before one wrote it, that is the highest possible achievement
of the poet as poet ... The task of the poet, in making people
comprehend the incomprehensible, demands immense
resources of language; and in developing the language,
enriching the meaning of words and showing how much
words can do, he is making possible a much greater range
of emotion and perception for other men, because he gives
them the speech in which more can be expressed.

(T.S. Eliot *What Dante means to me*)[157]

The same evolving conversation is engaged with the Upanishads in
Eliot's poem. 'The Upanishads are a series of commentaries on the
Vedas, ancient Sanskrit texts from the fifteenth to the fifth century BCE. The religion based on these ancient texts evolved into
Hinduism, and the texts became the sacred literature of that religion'.
The response to each incantation of DA in the poem is a Sanskrit
word, a sacred ancient language of India. The name derives from *sam-
skrtam*, meaning to put together, well-formed, and perfected, as befits
the language of the gods.[158] Inherent in both the language itself and
in the Upanishads is the theme of shaping humanity — Upanishad
meaning both to sit with a teacher, and to connect. Within that, the
theme of guidance is important, and the western version of this idea
is figuratively represented in Eliot's poem in the conjoining of the
Hellenic Sappho with the Hebraic Aaron.

The repetitive incantation of DA at the close of *The Waste Land*
echoes the repetitive beat of the comma in the opening of the poem.
The guide in the Upanishad of *The Waste Land* responds to a series
of questions from disciples with the same utterance, DA. In each
case the response elicits a different word, the *Datta, Dayadhvam* and

Damyata of Eliot's poem. Termed the 'Three Great Disciplines', they are explained by the Upanishad guide. 'That very thing is repeated even today by the heavenly voice, in the form of thunder, as "Da," "Da," "Da," which means: "Control yourselves," "Give," and "Have compassion." Therefore one should learn these three: self-control, giving, and mercy'.[159]

In its meaning 'to divide', *dā-* is the root of demography, democracy and demagogue. A suggested suffixed form *dā-mo-*, speculated to mean 'division of society', may even suggest the primeval beginnings of social demarcations and divisions. *dā-* is also the root of demotic, demon, and pandemonium, the 'hubbub wide' of Pandemonium, Milton's capital city of Hell he modelled in part on the biblical city of Babel, visited in the first book of this series. Conversely, as the root of 'demotic French' [212] it suggests a shared language such as the 'language of the Franks', a lingua franca that in earlier times was the demotic Greek of the Mediterranean, the language of the New Testament of the Bible. Resonating with other binary oppositions in the poem, DA in its divisive meaning is in each instance followed by a communally bonding alternative in '*Datta*, *Dyadhvam, Damyata*'.

It does seem that the Sanskrit words Eliot chose for the ending of his poem contain within them a choice made in favour of community. In that, a choice is also made for the type of person who, for the sake of that community, exercises self-control, generosity and human decency. As such, it echoes Eliot's Classicism and the *via media*, the middle way, inherent in which is the quality of empathy for fellow humans. Schopenhauer, not a believer, made a similar comparison of religions.

A religion which demands the greatest sacrifices, and which has yet remained so long in practice in a nation that embraces so many millions of people, cannot be an arbitrarily invented whim, but must have its basis in human nature. But besides this, if we read the life of a Christian penitent or saint, and also that of a Hindu saint, we cannot cease to wonder at the harmony we find between them ... So much agreement in spite of such different times and peoples is a factual proof that what is expressed here is not, as trite optimists like to assert, an eccentricity and perversion of the mind, but an essential side of human nature, an aspect seldom seen only because of its excellence.

(Arthur Schopenhauer *The World as Will and Idea*)[160]

12. THE DRUNKEN HYMN: ANARCHY AND ORDER

Dionysus and Apollo

> Under the spell of the Dionysian it is not only the bond between man and man that is re-established: nature in its estranged, hostile, or subjugated forms also celebrates its reconciliation with its prodigal son, man ... Now, with the gospel of world-harmony, each man feels himself not only reunified, reconciled, reincorporated, and merged with his neighbour, but genuinely one ... In song and dance man expresses himself as a member of a higher communal nature.
>
> (Friedrich Nietzsche *The Birth of Tragedy*)[161]

James Frazer and Jane Harrison link Dionysus, one of the earliest dying gods, to the dying gods of the wider ancient Mediterranean, an early milestone on the continuum in their work, and in Eliot's poem, that leads to the Christian Christ. Harrison sees the Alleluia of the Christian Easter Hymn as an echo of the Dionysian cultic exclamation, a 'homage beyond articulate speech' (here as Iacchos). 'Some, like Iacchos and probably Bacchos itself, though they ultimately became proper names, were originally only cries ... How many people attach any precise significance to the thrice repeated, stately and moving words that form the prooemium to our own Easter Hymn? 'Alleluia, Alleluia, Alleluia''. She makes that comparison in the same way she sees a comingling of art and ritual arise from humankind's earliest consciousness, so that it is 'at the outset one and the same impulse that sends a man to church and to the theatre'.[162] From the opening of *The Waste Land*, considerations of the ego, of the individual's relationship to society, and the tension between communal order and a primal taste for destruction, are figuratively shown to arise from the outset of humanity.

We have seen the aspect of the opening of *The Waste Land* that represents dance, showing the iamb and trochee to represent primeval human beats in poetry. As Eliot makes use of ancient metrical units of the Western classical tradition, so too he seems to engage on the level of form. While it is elevated poetics, it is not merely abstract literary discourse, addressing as it does the primal instinct for anarchic iconoclasm that is often twinned with and disguised within zealot reformation. Through form, the proposed destruction needed to establish a new world order inherent in Nietzsche's idea of Dionysian man is examined. The poem interrogates cultural and political currents in modernity, including egoism, using the tension between the anarchic Dionysian and the ordered Apollonian in poetry, showing that the zealot is sometimes disguised as the dancer.

As an aside on form, necessarily light touch as this is early research, the unified form that underlies the pseudo-anarchy of the poem, when hopefully revealed more fully over time, will no doubt be significantly complex. Within that, the map of poetry that is likely to commence from the opening seems to be expressed not only in meter and line, but also in stanza form, in that the two opening verse paragraphs seem to represent the Hellenic and Hebraic respectively. Where the first engages with classical myth, and classical forms such as the sapphic stanza and the Greek chorus, the imagery of the second is in the main that of the Bible. Within that, there is parallelism, a fundamental signature of Hebrew poetry. Notably, close to 'a third of the Hebrew Bible is poetry' and, further notable for *The Waste Land*, 'the most salient feature of biblical poetry, like the Semitic, and especially Ugaritic (13th century North Canaanite) poetry that preceded it, is *parallelismus membrorum* (Lowth) or parallelism'.[163] In Hebrew parallelism, the matter addressed is repeated in slightly different but resonating form, and serves, among other purposes, for emphasis. In Eliot's poem, that parallelism, centred on the 'red rock', is prominent in the second verse paragraph.

> There is no shadow under this red rock,
> (Come in under the shadow of this red rock),
> And I will show you something different from either
> Your shadow at morning striding behind you
> Or your shadow at evening rising to meet you;
> I will show you fear in a handful of dust.
>
> (*The Waste Land* 25 -30)

Close analysis is beyond the scope of this book, not least because the reverberating meanings here are compounded by Eliot's underlying poem, *The Death of St. Narcissus*. Three aspects can be mentioned. It may in part indicate a legacy of older oral culture, since in 'ritual poetries, repetition has a performative function ... Oral poems are repeated by being passed from generation to generation as well as structured by repetition that serves as a mnemonic device'.[164] The character in that poem, (like many in Eliot's poems, traversing time), because he 'could not live men's ways ... became a dancer before God', suggesting very ancient ritual forms; and this is repeated later in the poem. 'So, he became a dancer to God'.[165] Further, this Hebraic verse paragraph of *The Waste Land* ends with the 'handful of dust' from which Adam is created in the Book of Genesis, the name Adam being closely linked to the Hebrew words for 'red' and 'ground'. This biblical story of genesis, interwoven with the genesis of dance, music, culture and Hellenic myth that opens the poem, combines the Hellenic and Hebraic — culture and morality, reason and faith, art and spirituality, philosophy and theology — from the outset. Later again that duality is represented in Part III of the poem in the conjoining of the guides Sappho and Aaron.

To return to ancient Greek poetry, the most ancient Greek poetic forms are the anarchic dithyramb, the ordered paean and the satirical iambus. The dithyrambic wildness teeming in the opening of *The Waste Land* — nature goddesses, the muses of mounts Helicon and Olympia, hunting, feasting and dancing humans, and nymphs pursued by hoofed gods — can be contrasted to the marked discipline of its poetic form, more like the paean. The dithyramb and iambus have an overlapping heritage from the poetics of prehistoric times: 'we realise that iambic verse and the dithyrambic song are the final stages of a development whose beginning lies beyond our scope'. Versnal also notes that it 'is not a coincidence that the woman whose jests cheered the sad Demeter was called Iambē. It is especially in the ritual, satirical and abusive songs that the cults of Demeter and Dionysos overlap', and that the 'satirical character of the oldest iambs' resemble poetry 'typical of the Dionysiac cult'. That perspective was also available to Eliot from the work of Jane Harrison. 'Harrison points to the fact that the dithyramb is especially connected with Dionysos as the bull-god, the shape in which he preferably manifests himself'.[166]

The opening of the poem, relying heavily on the ancient simplicity of the iamb, invokes the iambus and Iambē. The iambus is funny, satirical and at times vituperative. According to Homer, Iambē was the irreverent woman who cheered the goddess Demeter as she sat grieving at the loss of her daughter Persephone, who had been abducted by Hades while gathering 'hyacinths' [35] by a river. As an entertainment muse to Demeter, Iambē joins the other muses who open *The Waste Land*, and 'is a personification of the iambic tradition, which reflects a ritual discourse that provokes laughter and thereby promotes fertility'.

> Unsmiling, not partaking of food or drink,
> she sat there, wasting away with yearning for her daughter
>   with the low-slung waistband,
> until Iambē, the one who knows what is dear and what is not,
>   started making fun.
> Making many jokes, she turned the Holy Lady's disposition in
>   another direction,
> making her smile and laugh and have a merry *thūmos* [heart].
> Ever since, she [Iambē] has been pleasing her with the
>   sacred rites.
>
> (Homer *Hymn to Demeter*)[167]

Iambē directs the reader to those aspects of *The Waste Land* that are funny — there are bitingly good literary jokes in the poem. She suggests a darkly satirical, even vituperative aspect to Eliot's poem as a response to vituperative scribes such as Milton and Nietzsche. Iambē is in good company, joining the fierce author of the *Satyricon*. That earthy, satirical work of classical Rome, recounting a society of extraordinary decadence and degeneracy, provides the epigraph to Eliot's poem, the sibyl trapped in a bell jar. We have seen how that resonates with Nietzsche's remarkable characterisation of the human ego as the 'wretched bell jar of individuality'. In that way, consideration of the human ego is engaged from the outset, and that includes in poetic form.

Dithyrambic verse was often (or said to be) composed and recited under the influence of wine as a more free-form celebration of the wilder attributes of human life, and in modern usage 'characterises a style that is ecstatic, vehement, or unpredictable'. The poet Archilochus wrote 'I know how to lead the beautiful dithy-ramb song of Lord Dionysus when my mind is thunder-struck with wine'.[168] The paean is the more sober and controlled salutation to Apollo, sometimes recited when going into battle. It is said to be derived from the god of healing Paian, physician to the Olympian gods, later linked with Apollo and Asclepius, god of medicine. Paian's name derives from 'to touch' in a healing sense, and he is said to save people from catastrophe. In such light, the paean can be a song of praise, a battle chant, and a healing hymn.

Whether it can be said that Eliot's opening is in part a paean remains to be determined. One form of the paean is thought to have been an antiphonal choral ode similar to the strophe and antistrophe in which, broadly, a group responds with simple phrases to a leader's recitals. It bears repeating that this is a sig-nificant form in Christian liturgy. In the classical world, it was often accompanied by the kithara, the instrument of Apollo and of Sappho, who was a lauded kitharode. According to Nietzsche, the 'music of Apollo was Doric architecture rendered in sound, but in the merely suggestive notes characteristic of the cithara. Carefully kept at a distance is precisely that element which defines the char-acter of Dionysian music and so of music itself, the shattering force of sound, the unified flow of melody and the utterly incomparable world of harmony'.[169]

In contrast to Nietzsche's preference for Dionysus and his reti-nue of satyrs, aspects such as the adonic fourth line of *The Waste Land* — the close of a sapphic stanza — suggest that the struc-ture of the opening of the poem is aligned with the ordered world of Apollo, embodied in Eliot's Classicism. Yet what Eliot creates within those ordered poetics is the corybantic world of Diony-sian play that we now know exists in the opening of his poem. It both mirrors and melds the tension Nietzsche highlights between the anarchic Dionysian world and the ordered Apollonian. Eliot's structural control intimates that humanity can enjoy all the dance and imaginative play it wants without sacrificing culture and civilisation, without tipping into the primal appetite for destruction. Nietzsche's addition of an accompanying antagonism between the sexes is predictable. 'The further development of art is just as dependent on their antagonism as the further development of mankind is dependent on the antagonism between the sexes'.[170] The reader sees how that plays out in the male and female duality of the fragmented layer of Eliot's poem.

A tension within the Dionysian exists in Nietzsche's work. The gap is marked between the cathartic, bonding, communal aspect of the Dionysian he expresses in *The Birth of Tragedy* and his later deployment of the Dionysian as a form of enjoyed anarchic cultural destruction to clear the path for his overman. Contemptuous of degenerate modernity, the later Nietzsche insists on a deliberately destructive reformation to reconfigure society and culture in favour of a pseudo-aristocratic cabal of overmen. In that way, his early mythic considerations later give way to the strident egoism of his overman, who represents, for the vast majority of the populace to be pressganged into his service, a joyless and ruthless puritanism in Dionysian costume. We will look at Nietzsche's faux neo-paganism shortly.

That tension is also marked in *The Waste Land*. Eliot wrote that it 'is perfectly obvious that art hangs between chaos on one side and mechanics on the other'.[171] The contrast between the Dionysian and the Apollonian is the contest between chaos and order, and between the middle way and zealotry, embedded in the poem from its outset. That is the figurative genesis of human culture, marking the emergence of a perpetual negotiation between the individual and society. Though Eliot may not concur with aspects of Nietzsche's distinction between the Dionysian and the Apollonian, he does seem to engage with it, since it is within the capability of his poetics, and the contrast resonates with his distinction between Romanticism and Classicism. He shows the one — dance, enjoyment and other temporary releases from the 'prison' [413] of the self — can be achieved without the destruction of community, of order.

According to Nietzsche in modernity, the anarchy inherent in the dithyramb is a figurative representation of the necessarily iconoclastic reformation that prepares the ground for his overman as the new man of the future. In contrast, the opening of *The Waste Land* is rigorously controlled within Eliot's classical style, more akin to the control of the ancient paean. This despite that, as we now know, the opening of the poem is a near riotous textual festival of dance, drama and recitals, teeming with human and mythic life. Although of high seriousness in its purpose, we might recall Iambē: there seems a pseudo-anarchic dark humour in the fact that the poem then apparently disintegrates into babel, its infamous fragmentation.

Nietzsche's Dionysian return to his preferred time of real men before Christianity and Socrates seems, in the context of Eliot's poem, a faux neo-paganism. *The Waste Land* celebrates the glories of womanhood, earthly and divine, before the grave scribal error of the creation of the Eve myth. Aphrodite, Mnemosyne and her daughters, Sappho, and the dancing and singing female celebrants of the *Vigil of Venus* all show an understanding of paganism as a fulsome incorporation of women in life, secular and divine.[172] That Eliot resurrects the Queen of Heaven in the Christian Mary is a complex reincarnation which, for the sake of focus, cannot be addressed here, save for the reminder that the origin of the Greek Aphrodite is in the Semitic Queen of Heaven of the southern Mediterranean. As Mary, she is always central to Eliot's consideration of the divine, and his consideration of women. Whereas Nietzsche's Dionysian perspective seems more cloven-footed. Linked as the overman is to Milton's Satan of the carbuncle eyes through the 'young man carbuncular' [231], he is the continuation of the satyr and Pan, whose wilful lust forces the chaste Syrinx to a form of suicide.

This contrast can be seen in Nietzsche's opinion of Napoleon, one of his prized templates for the overman. Much removed from the 'higher communal nature' of his first book, in *The Will to Power* he claims that 'for the sake of such a prize we should be willing to see our entire civilisation collapse into anarchy'. He also wrote that with '*Napoleon* we begin to comprehend that the superior and the formidable man form a necessary unity. The 'male' is restored; woman once again receives the contempt and fear she deserves'.[173] It bears repeating that, in contrast to his Dionysian advocacy, Nietzsche was not known to drink or dance, was rigorously ordered in his life and diet, and almost entirely withdrew from the modern society he considered degenerate to complete his works. 'Sexuality, ambition, the pleasure derived from illusion and deception, great joyous gratitude towards life and its typical conditions — that is what is essential to pagan cults and has a good conscience on its side'.[174] Yet he lived a strictly ascetic life antithetical to the Dionysian, a perpetual if unwilling celibate who imagines forms of intensified potency and control that might be effected on the world and women.

The dithyramb has not been as successful through history as classical poetry such as that of Sappho. 'Although hymns to Bacchus continued to be written, the genre of the dithyramb was moribund by the 2nd century BCE'.[175] In the late 1880s Nietzsche composed a set of *Dionysos-Dithyramben* that include his motifs of eagles, abysses and attestations to his struggles and greatness, which he dispersed among his prose works. In his opinion he did the world an enormous favour in doing so. 'Inasmuch as I want to do mankind a boundless favor, I give them my dithyrambs'.[176] Like his misogyny,

his poetry offers an easy target. When Eliot enwraps all the corybantic fun of the dithyramb in the classical Apollonian control and
Sapphic beauty of his opening verse, he undermines the need for
dithyrambic literary histrionics. That includes modern prose forms
such as Nietzsche's *Thus Spoke Zarathustra*. 'Confusion of thought,
emotion, and vision is what we find in such a work as *Also Sprach
Zarathustra*; it is eminently not a Latin virtue.'[177]

> God on the Cross is a curse upon Life, a signpost directing
> people to deliver themselves from it; — Dionysus cut into
> pieces is a promise of Life: it will be forever born anew and
> rise afresh from destruction.[178]

So Nietzsche ends *The Will to Power*. That aspect of secular thought
systems that is creed-like is reflected in the secular hymn Eliot noted
in his 1914 address to the Harvard Philosophical Club: 'there are
of course books and books with theories to account for the present misery — biological, sociological, economic ... and to hymn
the coming liberation and the fundamental goodness of man.
All this is natural enough. What interests me is not the uncritical
character of this cerebration, but its uncritical attempt to be critical, its feeling of the need for law at the same that it denies law;
its demand for a philosophy of the lawless, an intellectual justification for anti-intellectualism, a metaphysical justification of its blind
enthusiasm.'[179]

The Dionysian dithyramb is in part a hymn, and the ancient
drunken aspect of the dithyramb can be connected with the 1920s
through another aspect of Eliot's poem, again revealing the poem's
underlying unity. That connection is to Hermann Hesse's 'drunken
hymn', the babel of the European population as it reels towards
a repetition of the anarchy of the First World War. Nietzsche sees

his cultural reformation as a Dionysian dance that includes permission for any level of iconoclastic destruction necessary to prepare the way for his overman. Eliot sees Nietzsche as a heresiarch beating a drum for a dance of destruction with dark appeal to the innermost primal drives of man. That Dionysian iconoclastic drive encouraged by Nietzsche might be said to be drunk with zealotry. One aspect of the drunken hymn of Hermann Hesse is his warning of a populace blind to the threatened disintegration of Europe to which we are guided in the Notes. 'Cf. Hermann Hesse *Blick ins Chaos*' [366-76n] — In Sight of Chaos.

> *Already half Europe, at all events half Eastern Europe, is on the road to Chaos. In a state of drunken illusion she is reeling into the abyss and, as she reels, she sings a drunken hymn ....*[180]

NOTES

1 Don Gifford and Robert J. Seidman *Ulysses Annotated* (University of California Press 2008); Sam Slote, Marc A. Mamigonian and John Turner *Annotations to James Joyce's Ulysses* (Oxford University Press 2022).

2 T.S. Eliot 'Clark Lecture I' *The Complete Prose of T. S. Eliot: The Critical Edition: The Perfect Critic, 1919–1926* Vol 2 Eds. Anthony Cuda and Ron Shuchard (Baltimore: Johns Hopkins University Press and Faber & Faber Ltd 2014) p. 620. Hereafter CP2.

3 *The Letters of T.S. Eliot* Vol. 1 revised edition, Eds. Valerie Eliot, Hugh Haughton and John Haffenden (Faber & Faber 2009) p. 110. Hereafter, Letters 1.

4 T.S. Eliot 'American Literature and the American Language' *The Complete Prose of T. S. Eliot: The Critical Edition: A European Society, 1947–1953* Eds. Iman Javadi and Ronald Schuchard (Baltimore: Johns Hopkins University Press, 2018) p. 805. Hereafter CP7.

5 Letters 1.111.

6 Hugh Kenner *The Invisible Poet T.S. Eliot* (Methuen & Co. 1965) p. 63.

7 Langdon Hammer, Yale Courses, Modern Poetry 310, Lecture 8 Imagism, Chapter 1. Yale.edu.

8 The *Pervigilium Veneris*, a poem of late antiquity describing a three-day festival of Venus in April. See the first book in this series, *A Modern Eve*, hereafter referred to as book 1.

9 H.D. *Hymen* (Henry Holt and Company New York 1921) p. 7-15.

10 *Valerie Eliot The Waste Land: A Facsimile and Transcript of the Original Drafts* (London: Faber & Faber 1971) p.29, 41.

11 Friedrich Nietzsche *Thus Spoke Zarathustra* Trans. Graham Parkes (Oxford University Press 2008) Book I, §2, p. 67.

12 Matthew Hollis *A Biography of a Poem* (Faber & Faber 2022) p.145, 130.

13 T.S. Eliot 'London Letter' in *The Dial* October 1921, CP2.369.

14 Hollis *A Biography of a Poem* p. 274.

15 Gifford and Seidman *Ulysses Annotated* (University of California Press 2008) p.408.14.2, *Ulysses* 14.2, *Ulysses Annotated* 408 fn.1., 14.1.

16 Helen Gardner 'The Price of Modernism: Publishing *The Waste Land*' in *The Waste Land* Norton Critical Edition Ed. Michael North (W. W. Norton 2001) p.89.

17 T.S. Eliot 'Tradition and the Individual Talent' CP2.106.

18 'Tradition and the Individual Talent' CP2.107.

19 R. R. Marett *The Threshold of Religion* (Methuen & Co. Ltd) 2nd. ed. 1914, p.203-4.

20 'The Interpretation of Primitive Ritual' 1913. CP1.111. 'How far is it workable to regard a religion as a form of social behavior? This definition is accepted by Marett, and is quite in line with the tendencies of Durkheim'.

21 See book 1.

22 Jason Harding 'T.S. Eliot and *The Egoist*' in *T.S. Eliot and the Concept of Tradition* Eds. Giovanni Cianci and Jason Harding (Cambridge University Press 2007) p.94, 96-7.

23   Edward Tylor *Primitive Culture: Researches Into The Development Of Mythology, Philosophy, Religion Language, Art, And Custom* (London, John Murray, Albemarle Street, 1920) p. 425. See book 1.

24   Marrett *The Threshold of Religion* p. xi.

25   Marrett *The Threshold of Religion* p.220.

26   See book 1.

27   William M. Barton *The Pervigilium Veneris* (Bloomsbury Academic 2020) p. 71.

28   T.S. Eliot 'The Beating of a Drum' CP2.473.

29   W. O. E. Oesterley *The Sacred Dance: A Study in Comparative Folklore* (Cambridge University Press 1923) p. xiv

30   'Introduction' CP1. xlix, xlvii.

31   Eliot 'The Interpretation of Primitive Ritual' CP1.112.

32   Eliot '*Savonarola: A Dramatic Poem*, by Charlotte Eliot', CP2.771-2.

33   Oesterley *The Sacred Dance* Preface 3, 8, Contents.

34   James Frazer *The Golden Bough* Ed. and Introduction Robert Fraser (Oxford University Press 2009) p.327.

35   Fredrich Nietzsche *Daybreak* Trans. R.J. Hollingdale Eds. Maudemarie Clark and Brian Leiter (Cambridge University Press 2019) Bk I, § 70.

36   Christine Hayes, Yale Lectures transcript, RLST 145: *Introduction to the Old Testament (Hebrew Bible)*, Ch. 1.

37   Ovid *Metamorphoses* Trans. and Ed. Charles Martin (Norton Critical Edition 2010) p.75.

38   Virgil *The Aeneid* Trans. Michael J. Oakley (Wordsworth Classics 2002) Book I, I.728-45.

39   Saint Augustine *Confessions* Trans. Henry Chadwick (Oxford University Press 2008) p.91.

40   Virgil *The Aeneid* Book I, 491-8, P.16

41   William G. Dever *Did God Have a Wife?* (Wm. B. Eerdmans 2005) p. 99.

42   Israel Finkelstein and Neil Asher Silberman *The Bible Unearthed* (Touchstone / Simon and Schuster 2002) p. 118.

43   *The Bible Unearthed* p. 248-9.

44   Dever p. 67, 61.

45   Hugh Kenner *The Pound Era* (Pimlico 1991) p.96. First published 1971.

46   See in book 1.

47   Sir James George Frazer *Folk-Lore In The Old Testament. Studies In Comparative Religion: Legend And Law* Vol. 1 (MacMillan 1918) p.374. Leopold Bloom in *Ulysses* holds to a quasi-theological theory of the Ireland at that time: that Hebrew was the *Ur*-language of ancient Irish, connected through a king of Scythia who, it was theorised, was an ancestor of the Phoenicians who first occupied Spain and then ancient Ireland (U.17.724-773; UA.577.748).

48   An often-quoted statement of Millet, not precisely referenced. Endre Bojt in *Foreword to the Past: A Cultural History of the Baltic People* (Central European University Press 1999) cites 'Sabaliauskas 1986, 18' (p.79 fn.1).

49   John Miles Foley. *Traditional Oral Epic: The Odyssey, Beowulf, and the Serbo-Croation Return Song*. (Berkeley: University of California Press 1990) p.54.

50   *The Classical Review* Volume 38, Issue 1-2, February 1924, pp. 20 — 22.
51   Louis H. Gray University of Nebraska March 1, 1924, Book Review.
52   M. L. West 'Indo-European Meter' *Glotta* 51 3/4 (1973) pp. 161-187. p.161.
53   'Language trees with sampled ancestors support a hybrid model for the origin of Indo-European languages' Editor Summary, Science.org, 28 Jul 2023, Vol 381, Issue 6656, quoting the work of Paul Heggarty and Collaborators.
54   Robert Beekes *Etymological Dictionary of Greek* (Brill, Leiden, Boston 2010). From the Leiden Indo-European Etymological Dictionary Series, Ed. Alexander Lubotsky.
55   See book 1.
56   Friedrich Nietzsche *The Birth of Tragedy* Trans. Douglas Smith (Oxford University Press 2008) p. 39.
57   T.S. Eliot 'London Letter' in *The Dial* October 1921, CP2.369.
58   George Saintsbury *A History of English Prosody* (MacMillan and Co. 1908) p. 401.
59   https://en.wikipedia.org/wiki/Iamb_(poetry)
60   *The Princeton Encyclopaedia of Poetry & Poetics* 4th edition. Editor in Chief. Roland Greene, Gen ed. Stephan Cushman, Associate Eds. Clare Cavanagh, Jahan Ramazani and Paul Rouzer; Assist. Eds. Harris Feinsod, David Marno and Alexandra Slessarev (Princeton University Press 2012) p. 652. Hereafter *Princeton*.
61   Antoine Meillet *Les Origines indo-européennes des Mètres Grecs* (Les Presses Universitaires des France 1923) p.19. (Translated).
62   CP1.513.
63   Meillet p.55-6. // & *The Classical Review*, Volume 38, Issue 1-2, February 1924, pp. 20 — 22
64   How bipedalism created music | Michael Spitzer — YouTube.
65   *Sweeney Among the Nightingales* 1, *Sweeney Erect* 21. See also *Mr. Eliot's Sunday Morning Service* "Sweeney shifts from ham to ham", 29.
66   Etymonline.com: also enjambement, 1837, from French enjambement or from enjamb (c. 1600), from French enj"mber "to stride"over," from en- (see en- (1)) + "amb" "leg" (see jamb).
67   Oesterley *The Sacred Dance* — see essay three, 'The Primal Dance'.
68   Michael Spitzer *The Musical Human* (Bloomsbury 2022) p.10.
69   Spitzer *The Musical Human* (Bloomsbury 2022) pp.327-330.
70   CNN: Mysterious species buried their dead and carved symbols 100,000 years before humans.
71   T.S. Eliot *The Beating of a Drum* 1923, CP2.473, quoting "(Butcher, 139)".
72   40,000 years of music explained in 8 minutes | Michael Spitzer — YouTube.
73   Spitzer *The Musical Human* (Bloomsbury 2022) p 326-7.
74   Harrison *Ancient Art and Ritual* Chapter II, 'Primitive Ritual: Pantomimic Dances', p.42.
75   Spitzer *The Musical Human* (Bloomsbury 2022) p. 319, 322.
76   Jürgen Habermas *The Philosophical Discourse of Modernity* Trans. Fredrick Lawrence (Polity Press 1987) p. 97, 94.
77   Nietzsche *The Birth of Tragedy* Trans. Smith, p.47.
78   Jane Harrison *The Religion of Ancient Greece* (Constable & Co, London 1913) p.11.
79   *Ulysses* 15.2091.

80   V. *Pervigilium Veneris* [428n]. See book 1

81   In Book 1, the 'sun's last rays' [225] are read with Friedrich Nietzsche's declaration of the death of God in the late nineteenth century: 'some kind of sun seems to have set; some old, deep trust turned into doubt ... This long, dense succession of demolition, destruction, downfall, upheaval that now stands ahead: who would guess enough of it to play the teacher and herald of this monstrous logic of horror, the prophet of deep darkness and eclipse of the sun the like of which has probably never before existed on earth?' Friedrich Nietzsche *The Gay Science* Book V, §343, p.199.

82   *Princeton* p. 1254.

83   James A. Notopoulos 'Mnemosyne in Oral Literature' in *Transactions and Proceedings of the American Philological Association* Vol. 69 (1938), pp. 465-493, pp. 465-466. He quotes H. J. Rose.

84   Friedrich Nietzsche *The Birth of Tragedy* Trans. Shaun Whiteside, Ed. Michael Tanner (Penguin 2003) p. 36.

85   See book 1.

86   Hollis *A Biography of a Poem* p. 283-4.

87   *Ulysses Annotated* p. 2.

88   Jason Harding 'Unravelling Eliot' *The New Cambridge Companion to T.S. Eliot* Ed. Jason Harding (Cambridge University Press 2017) p.1 3.

89   T.S. Eliot *Choruses from 'The Rock'* in *The Poems of T.S. Eliot: Vol. I*, Christopher Ricks and Jim McCue (Faber & Faber 2015) p. 168: VII:4-25.

90   Jessie L. Weston *From Ritual to Romance* (Dover Publications 1997) Contents, p. x — xi.

91   Weston *From Ritual to Romance* p. 120-1.

92   Ricks and McCue *The Poems of T.S. Eliot* p. 589.

93   Fredrich Nietzsche *Ecce Homo* Trans. R.J. Hollingdale (Penguin Books 2004) p. 82.

94   Friedrich Nietzsche *The Gay Science* Ed. Bernard Williams (Cambridge University Press 2001) Book III, §124, p. 119.

95   Arthur C. L. Brown 'The Bleeding Lance' (*Modern Language Association of America* 1910) Vol. XXV, 1, p.1.

96   Weston *From Ritual to Romance*, Contents.

97   Weston *From Ritual to Romance*, Preface vi-vii.

98   Ricks and McCue *The Poems of T.S. Eliot* p. 590.

99   BBC: 'Ancient DNA sheds light on Irish origins'.

100   BBC: 'Stonehenge: DNA reveals origin of builders'.

101   Jane Ellen Harrison *The Religion Of Ancient Greece* (Constable & Company 1913) p. 26.

102   Weston *From Ritual to Romance* p. 121.

103   *Ulysses* 3.35.

104   *Ulysses Annotated* p. 12.

105   *Ulysses* 1.85, 3.31, 14.296 as 'Mighty Mother', and in other forms throughout.

106   *Ulysses* 15.2096.

107   Jewel Spears Brooker *Mastery and Escape: T. S. Eliot and the Dialectic of Modernism* (University of Massachusetts Press 1994) p. 31.

108 *Ulysses* 17.1026.

109 *Ulysses* 1.708, *Ulysses Annotated* 1.708.

110 Robert Spoo *James Joyce and the Language of History: Dedalus's Nightmare* (Oxford University Press -1994) p. 21, referencing '(Letters 1 54-56)'. *Ulysses* 14.1467.

111 *Ulysses* 2.362, 4.1-5; *Ulysses Annotated* p. 70, fn1; *Ulysses* 4.10.

112 *Ulysses* 1.2; 1.585; *Ulysses Annotated* 1.3.

113 *Ulysses Annotated* 1.2.

114 John Milton *Paradise Lost* Book IV, Book X.

115 *Ulysses* 8.297.

116 T.S. Eliot 'Knowledge and Experience in the Philosophy of F. H. Bradley' in *The Complete Prose of T. S. Eliot: The Critical Edition: Apprentice Years, 1905–1918* Eds. Ronald Schuchard and Jewel Spears Brooker (Baltimore: Johns Hopkins University Press and Faber & Faber Ltd 2014) p. 274.

117 Virginia Woolf *A Room of One's Own* (Penguin 2000) p. 37.

118 *Ulysses* 17.2042-2058; *Ulysses Annotated* 17.2046.

119 David Lyle Jeffrey *A Dictionary of Biblical Tradition in English Literature* (Wm. B. Eerdmans Publishing Co. 1992) p.802. Referring to '*Paradise Lost* (6.761; cf. 3.596-601)', '*Reason of Church Government* (1.5)', and '*Paradise Regained* (3.13-15)'.

120 *Ulysses Annotated* p. 1.2

121 *Ulysses* 12.608-624. Gifford notes that 'Emmet was hanged and beheaded, not hanged, drawn and quartered' Since his avatar Stephan Dedalus observes that a 'man of genius makes no mistakes. His errors are volitional and are the portals of discovery' (U.9.228), this is a deliberate error on Joyce's part. Deliberate error is also used in *The Waste Land*, so also creating 'portals of discovery'.

122 *Ulysses* 1.296, 8.10-13.

123 *Ulysses* 12.151-205.

124 See book 1 photographs. Tarot card imagery is also included in the poem, which is likely to represent ersatz spiritualism but may also serve to show the antiquity and longevity of that imagery. That aspect itself is complex and so will be addressed elsewhere.

125 Dionysus-Dithyrambs, The Nietzsche Channel.com.

126 Harrison *The Religion of Ancient Greece* p. 11.

127 Hesiod Homeric Hymns and Homerica, Project Gutenberg.

128 Christopher Snow Hopkins 'Picturing Paradise: T. S. Eliot, John Milton, and Jean-Honoré Fragonard' www.frick.org/blogs/curatorial/

129 Christopher Ricks *T.S. Eliot Inventions of the March Hare: Poems 1909-1917* Ed. Christopher Ricks (Hardcourt Brace 1997) p. 151.

130 See book 1.

131 Ricks *T.S. Eliot Inventions of the March Hare: Poems 1909-1917* p. 27.

132 Charles Baudelaire *The Flowers of Evil (Les Fleurs du mal)* Trans. Aaron Poochigian, Introduction Dana Gioia, Afterword Daniel Handler (Liveright Publishing) 2022) p. 137-9.

133 See book 1.

134 CP1.xiv, General Editorial Introduction.

135   T.S. Eliot 'Baudelaire' 1930 CP4.157.

136   'Baudelaire in our Time' CP2.75. naturaliter: "anima naturaliter Christiana" [a naturally Christian soul], a phrase used by Tertullian in *Apologeticum* XVII.6.

137   John Henry Newman, Tractarian progenitor of Anglo-Catholicism, *Tract 4*, 1833.

138   T.S. Eliot 'The Lesson of Baudelaire' *The Tyro: A Review of the Arts of Painting, Sculpture, and Design* (Spring 1921) CP2.306.

139   Charles Baudelaire *Intimate Journals* Trans. Christopher Isherwood, (Methuen & Co. 1949) p. 61.

140   Baudelaire *Intimate Journals* p. 58.

141   Frank R. Blake 'The Origin of pronouns of the First and Second Person' *The American Journal of Philology* Vol. 55, No. 3 (1934), pp. 244-248.

142   W. H. I. Bleek 'The Concord, the Origin of Pronouns, and the Formation of Classes or Genders of Nouns' The *Journal of the Anthropological Institute of Great Britain and Ireland* Vol. 1 (1872) pp. lxiv-xc.

143   W.B. Yeats 'The Celtic Element in Literature' Part III.

144   Laurence Rainey 'With Automatic Hand: *The Waste Land*' *The New Cambridge Companion to The Waste Land* Ed. Jason Harding (Cambridge University Press 2017) p. 73.

145   *The Poems of T.S. Eliot* p. 605.I:12.

146   See Appendix 7. The line also gives Eliot the opportunity to name the languages Russian, Lithuanian and German in what may be an ambition to name or allude to all the main languages of Europe and all the associated languages of Proto-Indo-European, such as Sanskrit. This is linked with the alphabet of Phlebas the Phoenician, civilisation's Adam, creating a map of the development of language and writing, to complement a possible map of the development of poetry, again mirroring the ambition of James Joyce in *Ulysses*.

147   See book 1.

148   Valerie Eliot *Facsimile and Transcript* p. 125-6.

149   Verlag Christian Brandstätter *Sisi Myth and Truth* (Grasl Druck & Neue Medien 2005) p. 88.

150   This essay also introduces Goethe's Faust and the Eternal Feminine to the poem, in the form of the *Faustian Muttern*.

151   Countess Marie Wallersee-Larisch *My Past* (Forgotten Books 2012, originally published 1918) p. 54, 152.

152   Arthur Schopenhauer *The World as Will and Idea* Ed. David Berman, Introduction J.M. Dent (Orion Books 1995) p. 196.

153   Hugh Kenner *The Pound Era* (Pimlico 1991) p. 109.

154   Otto Jespersen *Language, Its Nature, Development and Origin* (George Allen & Unwin Ltd 1921) p. 7.

155   K. J. Phillips 'Jane Harrison and Modernism' *Journal of Modern Literature* Vol. 17, No. 4 Spring 1991 (Indiana University Press) p. 467, 473-4.

156   T.S. Eliot 'Tradition and the Individual Talent' *The Sacred Wood* (Faber and Faber 1997). First printed 1920. P. 41, 49.

157   T.S. Eliot 'What Dante means to me' *To Criticise the Critic* (Faber and Faber 1978) p. 133-4.

158 Etymology online; ahdictionary.com/word/indoeurop.html *dā-; Etymonline.com /word/demon

159 *The Waste Land* (Norton Critical Edition 2001) p. 62-3.

160 Schopenhauer *The World as Will and Idea* p. 244.

161 Nietzsche *The Birth of Tragedy* Trans. Smith p. 22-23.

162 Jane Harrison *Prolegomena to the study of the Greek Religion* (Cambridge: at the University Press 1908) p. 413; Jane Harrison *Ancient Art and Ritual* (Oxford University Press 1948) p. 9. First printed 1913.

163 *Princeton* 'Hebrew Poetry' p. 602.

164 *Princeton* p. 1169.

165 Ricks and McCue *The Poems of T.S. Eliot* p. 270-1, lines 17, 33.

166 H.S. Versnel *Triumphus* (Brill, Leiden 1970) p.16, 38. A book that argues for a very ancient, prehistoric origin for the Roman Triumph (victory procession).

167 chs.harvard.edu/primary-source/homeric-hymn-to-demeter-sb/#fn18

168 *Princeton* p. 370.

169 Nietzsche *The Birth of Tragedy* Trans. Smith p. 26.

170 Friedrich Nietzsche *The Will to Power* Trans. R. Kevin Hill and Michael A. Scarpitti. Ed. R. Kevin Hill (Penguin Classics 2017). §877, p. 501, §1050, p. 573.

171 T.S. Eliot 'Ezra Pound: His Metric and Poetry' *To Criticise the Critic* (Faber and Faber 1978) p. 171.

172 See book 1.

173 Nietzsche *The Will to Power* §877 p. 501, §1017 p. 559.

174 Nietzsche *The Will to Power* §1047, p. 572.

175 *Princeton* p. 371.

176 wikipedia.org/wiki/Dionysian_Dithyrambs; thenietzschechannel.com/works-pub /dd/dd.htm

177 T.S. Eliot 'William Blake' CP2.191.

178 Nietzsche *The Will to Power* §1052, p. 577.

179 T.S. Eliot 'The Relationship between Politics and Metaphysics' CP1.90-91.

180 Herman Hesse 'The Downfall of Europe' *The Waste Land* Ed. Michael North (Norton Critical Ed. 2001) p. 61.

Index